HOW TO BUILD HIGH-PERFORMANCE
IGNITION SYSTEMS

For Domestic and Import 4, 6, and 8-Cylinder Cars

TODD RYDEN

S·A DESIGN

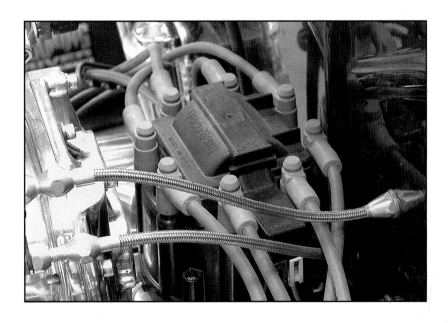

CarTech

Auto Books & Manuals

Edited By: Travis Thompson

ISBN 1-884089-72-0

Order No. SA79

Printed in China

CarTech®, Inc.,
39966 Grand Avenue
North Branch, MN 55056
Telephone (651) 277-1200 • (800) 551-4754 • Fax: (651) 277-1203
www.cartechbooks.com

OVERSEAS DISTRIBUTION BY:

Brooklands Books Ltd.
P.O. Box 146, Cobham, Surrey, KT11 1LG, England
Telephone 01932 865051 • Fax 01932 868803
www.brooklands-books.com

Brooklands Books Aus.
3/37-39 Green Street, Banksmeadow, NSW 2109, Australia
Telephone 2 9695 7055 • Fax 2 9695 7355

Front Cover (large): **There are a variety of aftermarket components available that will fire up your ignition system. Depending on your engine and application there are distributors, coils, multiple-sparking ignition controls, and spark plug wires. Examples shown here are from Accel, Mallory, Moroso, and MSD.**

Front Cover (upper): **This race car is equipped with an aftermarket electronic fuel-injection system from F.A.S.T., as well as a Programmable Ignition Control and coil from MSD.**

Front Cover (lower): **Late-model ignition systems that don't use a distributor can still be upgraded with aftermarket ignition products. In this application, the stock coil packs and plug wires have been upgraded with parts from MSD.**

Back Cover (left): **This LS-1 Chevy engine uses a coil for each cylinder. Replacing these coils for higher-output performance models is tough because the transistors that monitor the firing are built into each coil. This means you can't just swap out the coil for any replacement.**

Back Cover (right): **The best way to make modifications to a distributor is with the help of a distributor spin fixture. This way you can spin the distributor and put a timing light on each plug wire to determine the amount of timing change for each cylinder.**

Back Cover (large): **You can control when the ignition is triggered by moving the distributor (when it holds the trigger device). But there is much more to setting the ignition timing than simply setting the placement of the distributor while the engine is idling.**

TABLE OF CONTENTS

PREFACE AND ACKNOWLEDGMENTS

Thanks for purchasing *How to Build High-Performance Ignition Systems*! That is, unless you're just thumbing through while sitting in a fluffy chair at the bookstore waiting for your double-dipped espresso-capa-coffee to cool down. Either way, thanks for taking a look.

So what makes me qualified to write a book on high-performance ignition systems? I started in the performance automotive world like most anyone else — by being an enthusiast. I just happened to spend a decade involved in the performance ignition area of the performance aftermarket with one of the leading companies — MSD Ignitions — so I picked up a lot of useful information and experience. And now, I get to pass this info on in hopes that it answers a lot of the questions and troubles I've heard about through the years.

To many, the ignition system may cause anxiety or be intimidating. For those of you, I ask that you relax, because the idea was not to fill this book with engineering speak! I'm merely serving as an interpreter between you and the brains that do comprehend electrons, induction, milliHenrys, joules, and capaci-

tance. I prefer not to think about all the little things that have to happen on the circuit boards of these controls, and would rather take the time to explain the different parts and accessories you need to assemble and tune a great performing ignition system.

Before I got into this industry, I had many of the same questions about igni-

tions as you. I've stood in speed shops wondering if my mild 454 really needs a 60,000-volt coil. I've cracked my elbow on the hood hinge after grabbing the coil wire and getting shocked. I've set up timing wrong, burned up plug wires, and even shorted out a tachometer. In short, I've made many of the same mistakes that everyone else has, but maybe won't admit. Hopefully this book will answer your questions and help you avoid some of those mistakes.

So pull up a stool and kick your feet up on the tool box and let's bench race about ignitions. Thanks.

ACKNOWLEDGEMENTS

I owe a lot of thank-yous to a long list of people that helped me with this project.

To start with, I'd like to say thanks to the crew at Westech including Steve Brule, Tom Habrzyk, Rick Stoner, and John Baechtel, who talked me into this project (perhaps with a little prodding from Steve Hendrickson, the editor-in-chief at CarTech Books). I'd also like to thank all of the different companies that took the time to get me product information, photos,

stantly bother with questions about troubleshooting and ignition info. Also, thanks go to Jack and Sharon Priegel, Russell Stephens, Ed Monte, Spike Clapper, Jeff Gaul, Carole Bartlett, Joe Pando, Brandon Uhde, the graphics crew, engineers, service group, and everyone at ACC whom I've worked with for over a decade. It's been a great experience, and it's always been a group that I'm proud to be a part of.

As with any big project, there was plenty of support from behind the scenes. Michelle, thank you for understanding and putting up with this project (and many others). What would a page of acknowledgments be without a nod of appreciation to my folks and family for their support through all the years? Thank you for everything.

— *Todd*

Ignition manufacturers almost always offer different levels of ignition products for different levels of performance. Research can help you decide what you need for your application, or you could just call the manufacturer's tech line to see what they recommend.

and answers to my many questions that made this book possible. So a special thanks goes to Mike Golding, Shawn Umphries, and Mike Stasko at Mr. Gasket; Roy Griffith and Terry Johnson at Crane Cams; Kirk Haight at Electromotive; Don Ward of Autolite; Vince Sica at Powermaster; Mike Brown of Wires and Pliers; Rick Moroso and Ron Johnson at Moroso; Steve Davis of Performance Distributors; Mike Abney at Fire Control; and Jim Dindinger at Denso.

A huge thanks goes to Robert Martin for the great looking graphics and illustrations throughout the book. (Sorry about the last minute rush too.) There are several people from Autotronic Controls, including Rick Bennett and Mike Sharp, who I con-

No matter what you drive, the parts and tools to improve your car's ignition are out there. This book will give you the information you need to get the right parts and the best performance.

INTRO AND OVERVIEW
A Quick Look at the Entire System

It's the beginning of the book, so it's perfectly fitting to start with the basics of the ignition system before we get into performance goodies. The goal of an automotive ignition system is to produce a spark that will promote the combustion of the air/fuel mixture in a given cylinder. This is simplified to say the least. The spark that the ignition produces must have a high enough voltage to jump the spark plug gap, plus it must arrive in the cylinder at a near perfect moment in the combustion stroke of the piston. The spark occurs when the air/fuel mixture is being compressed. The mixture is ignited, resulting in a tremendous downforce on the piston, which creates a mechanical potential. The fact that the ignition system makes this all happen at the right moment, with a high-output spark, thousands of times in a minute, is something most of us take for granted. There's a lot of work taking place behind the scenes. Plus, there is a lot that can cause things to go wrong, which will rob your engine of performance. You need to assemble a reliable ignition system that will meet your engine's requirements.

An automotive ignition system operates by taking a low voltage with high current from the car's battery and changing it into a higher voltage with lower current to jump the spark plug

There are a lot of different components that go into an ignition system. This means that there are many ways to improve your ignition's performance by selecting components that offer improved accuracy, output, and strength.

gap and induce combustion in the cylinder. This process of changing low voltage to high voltage, called induction, takes place in the coil. From there, the distributor must get the spark to the right cylinder at the right moment.

Since electricity is not something we can physically hold, the ignition system has always presented a mystery to performance enthusiasts. Once you have a little better understanding on how the ignition works and what each component actually does, things will begin to make sense. There really are no magical or mysterious things happening in the ignition, although sometimes it may feel that way. Don't let the number of CD ignitions, distributors, and coils worry you. The fact that there are so many components available to improve your ignition's performance is a great thing, as it allows you to pick and choose the components that will provide you with the power you need for your car or truck.

Before you can plan an ignition system for your engine, you need to understand the fundamentals of a system and each of the main components. An ignition system needs to:

- Produce a high-voltage spark from a low voltage supply source (the battery)
- Distribute this spark to the combustion chamber at the opportune moment in the compression stroke of the piston
- Control and even change the moment that this spark occurs in the cylinder to meet different engine demands
- Be able to reliably accomplish these goals throughout a variety of operating conditions and changing temperatures

BREAKING THE IGNITION DOWN

A car's ignition system and its components can be broken down into two sides: a primary, and a secondary side.

The Primary Side

The primary side consists of components that operate with the low voltage from the battery. Note that all of these parts use conventional wiring, since they're carrying lower voltages. This includes the battery itself, the ignition switch, a switching device, an ignition control (when used), and the wiring leading to the coil's negative and positive terminals. The coil is the point where the primary and secondary systems meet, since a low voltage goes into the coil, but a high voltage comes out through the high-tension lead.

The Secondary Side

The high-voltage lead that comes out of the coil, commonly known as the coil wire, is connected to the distributor cap. From here, the high voltage, generally anywhere from 20,000 – 40,000 volts, races through the rotor tip and across a small gap to another cap terminal. From there it moves out of the cap, through a spark plug wire, and finally across the spark plug gap. The secondary side of the ignition requires high-voltage wiring with thick insulation, otherwise known as the spark plug wires. All of the components that make up the secondary side of the ignition are maintenance items and need to be checked throughout the cruising or racing season.

With the ignition divided in two, we'll break each side's components down even further to see how what each part is responsible for in each of these systems.

THE COIL

The ignition coil is an incredible part of the ignition system, and if there is any part that resembles a magical black box, it should be the coil. Think about it. The coil receives 12 volts from the battery, then outputs a spark that is 15,000 volts or higher! But like most things in the world, this phenomenon can be explained, and once you understand how this works, you can even attempt to tune your ignition with different coils. We'll get into coils in greater detail in Chapter 4. For now, we'll stick with explaining the magic

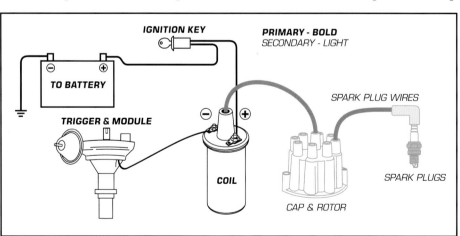

This chart shows a complete ignition system with the primary components in bold and the secondary components in gray. The primary side consists of components that deal with lower voltages, while the secondary deals with well over 15,000 volts and more!

There are many shapes and sizes of coils available for a variety of different ignitions. Engineers can manipulate the internals of coils to make higher voltage, more current, different spark duration, and more. Be sure to choose a coil to match your needs.

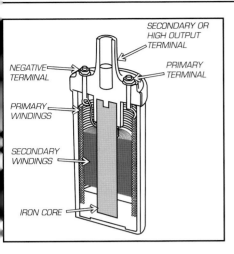

This cut-away canister coil shows the internals of the coil. There is a set of primary windings, an iron core to promote the magnetic field created, and a set of secondary windings.

they produce. It kind of falls into the primary and secondary sides of the ignition system, but is generally thought of as part of the secondary side.

The coil consists of two sets of windings made up of insulated wires that surround an iron core. The primary windings are generally made up of several hundred turns of a heavy wire. The secondary windings are made up of a much smaller gauge wiring and consist of thousands of turns. Coil manufacturers use a ratio between the secondary and primary winding numbers as a specification such as 100:1, which would mean 100 secondary turns to every one of the primary. This is a commonly used specification that can be useful when you begin trying to locate the best coil for your application.

When the switching device or trigger signal is closed in a typical factory-style inductive ignition, current from the battery flows through the thicker primary windings and a magnetic field builds in strength thanks to the help of the iron core. When the switching device opens (or is triggered), the flow of current is broken and its magnetic field collapses over to the thousands of secondary windings. During this collapse, the voltage is stepped up, creating the higher voltage that is required to jump the spark plug gap and ignite the air/fuel mixture.

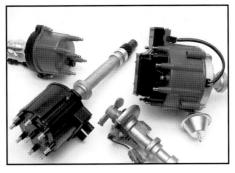

Distributors come in all shapes and sizes. Most are responsible for triggering the ignition as well as carrying the high voltage to the cylinders at the correct time. Before electronics controlled the timing, the distributor handled that chore as well.

DISTRIBUTOR

Like the coil, the distributor dabbles a little into the primary side of the ignition, but is very important and probably best known for its role in distributing the higher secondary voltage. The distributor generally houses the trigger mechanism that controls when the primary voltage collapses to the secondary windings of the coil.

Before any of this occurs though, the distributor shaft must be turned. In most cases, this is done by the engine's camshaft. There are two helically cut gears that mesh together to turn the distributor shaft. This rotation starts the triggering, the centrifugal advance (when equipped), and the high-voltage acceptance from the coil and the subsequent delivery through the cap's terminals. From there, the voltage travels through the spark plug wires and eventually reaches the plugs. There's a lot riding on and in the distributor, so pay attention when you're looking to upgrade.

TRIGGER DEVICE

There are several ways to trigger the ignition, but they all have the same goal: to break the flow of current into the coil resulting in a high voltage induced into the secondary side of the coil. This triggering method can be accomplished through mechanical

breaker points or different electronic variations. Age-old breaker points seem to provide the easiest method to grasp the operation of triggering the ignition.

Think of the breaker points as a simple on/off switch that is normally closed. While in the closed position, voltage from the battery flows into the primary windings because the closed points are providing a path to ground. When the points open, all of the current in the coil jumps ship to the secondary windings, where it eventually finds a ground path through the spark plug. As soon as the points close again, a ground path is returned and the battery current flows through the primary again. The amount of time that they're closed is referred to as dwell time.

Breaker points haven't been used in new cars for years, but they are still available in new aftermarket distributors. Electronic triggers that offer maintenance-free operation and improved trigger control replaced points in the mid 1970s.

All trigger designs share the common goal of signaling the ignition to release the high-voltage spark, they just take different routes to get there. In most cases, the trigger device is located inside the distributor, but there are exceptions to that rule. Most high-end drag cars and many late-model cars have systems that incorporate an external

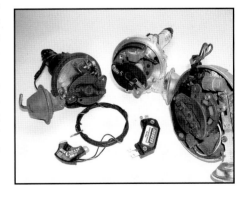

For most of the performance applications out there, a distributor is still responsible for triggering the ignition system. There are different versions of trigger sources ranging from mechanical points to magnetic pickups and Hall-effect switches, or even light-emitting diodes.

Detroit Goes Electronic

The big three domestic auto manufacturers all had their own electronic ignition by the mid 1970s. Chrysler stepped up to the plate first by installing electronic ignitions as standard equipment across the board in 1973. The systems used a magnetic pickup in the distributor with a small electronic controller to manage the dwell and flow of current to the coil. This system has gone through variations throughout the years but for the most part, the same system is still offered in their performance catalogs today. The distributor trigger is the same and there has probably been changes in the mechanical advance setup, but the real difference in design is in the ignition boxes they offer for different performance applications. Chrysler didn't want to be bothered with exciting marketing names, so they simply offer three different colored ignition boxes: Orange, Chrome, and Gold. The Orange is the basic street version; the Gold is the high-output race system; and the Chrome box lies somewhere in between.

Ford introduced the Duraspark electronic ignition in 1974, which, like the Chrysler design, used a magnetic pickup with an external ignition controller. In the later 1970s, this system was upgraded with components to improve the secondary voltage and longevity of the parts, including a larger diameter distributor cap. This upgrade was officially dubbed the Duraspark II. These distributors are still supplied on many of Ford's performance crate engines, plus they offer an Extra Performance Ignition Module that delivers increased spark energy and even has a built-in rev limiter.

The first mass-produced electronic distributor from the halls of General Motors was the High Energy Ignition (HEI) unitized distributor. HEI was on every GM product by 1975. Not only did this distributor incorporate a magnetic pickup design, but it also had the coil incorporated into its cap. Though the distributor is considerably bulky, it offers a single-wire hook-up, and there are no external components or other wiring. These benefits have kept the GM HEI system extremely popular among enthusiasts, and it is still widely used and supplied in many of the General's crate motors.

You can get performance ignition components right from the source. Most of the time, these higher-output ignition parts are sourced from the aftermarket. Mopar Performance Parts offers different ignition boxes for their distributors.

General Motors' integrated coil-in-cap distributor, known as the HEI, was a breakthrough in electronic distributor technology. You can find an assortment of performance parts and brand new HEI distributors for applications from street rods to racing.

trigger device on the crankshaft. This is commonly called a crank trigger. Even late-model systems that don't have a distributor all still require a switching method. It all started with mechanical breaker points, but there are much better electronic trigger devices that will not wear or require adjusting like points do. Magnetic pickups, Hall-effect switches, and optical trigger devices are just a few electronic trigger devices, and they will be covered more in the upcoming chapters.

TIMING

As with so many things that occur in life, timing is indeed everything — especially when you're dealing with ignition systems. The spark must jump the spark plug gap at the exact moment in order to achieve the best combustion event, and thus, the most force to push the piston down on the power stroke. If the spark occurs too late (is too retarded) in the compression stroke, the air/fuel mixture may not have time to fully combust, resulting in less force to push the piston. If it occurs too soon, the combustion event may occur too early resulting in pre-ignition, which will rob the engine of power and can even lead to damage. Pre-ignition is sometimes referred to as detonation.

To make matters worse, the ideal timing setting varies as engine RPM and load change. At lower RPM, the piston is traveling slower, so you need less time to burn the fuel. But at high RPM, the fuel must be ignited sooner in the pis-

ton's stroke to achieve the same burn. This can be done mechanically inside the distributor, or through a long list of electronic controls.

When the distributor is saddled with this chore, it is equipped with a mechanical advance assembly that operates through centrifugal force. Controlling how fast and how much the timing gets advanced is another tuning aspect that you get to set up for your application. While we're inside the distributor, there is another chore to add to its list of responsibilities. Whether or not the distributor triggers the ignition, it still has to perform the task that it was named after.

Distributing and the Secondary Side

The distributor also is labeled with the job of sending the spark from the coil to each of the spark plugs. This is done through the rotor and cap. The high voltage from the coil enters the cap through its center terminal. This terminal is different than the other terminals as it has a ball or tip inside the cap. This piece is generally made out of a long lasting, highly conductive material, because it is in constant contact with the rotor tang.

The rotor tang is generally bent up and away from the base of the rotor. This is either the entire rotor tip, or it joins into a thicker material for better spark transfer. The rotor tang is one area to watch for excessive pitting or signs of burning. When the rotor tip aligns with the distributor cap terminal, the spark should jump across to the terminal. Once the spark makes it across to the cap terminals, it's a simple run through the plug wire to the spark plug and across its gap. But like any path, there may be obstacles along the way.

SPARK PLUG WIRES

The spark plug wires are the arteries of the ignition system, as they provide a path for the sparks to flow through to get to the spark plugs. The importance of good quality spark plug wires cannot be stressed enough! Plug wires need to be able to live in a harsh environment and deal with high heat, abrasion, and getting whipped around

You can control when the ignition is triggered by moving the distributor (when it holds the trigger device). But there is much more to setting the ignition timing than simply setting the placement of the distributor while the engine is idling.

Distributorless Systems

This cut away distributor shows the relationship of the rotor tang with the center terminal of the distributor cap. It's important that they make contact, but too much contact can result in premature wear of the rotor.

Have you ever stopped to wonder how all of the trigger signals, timing, and delivery of spark would occur if there was no distributor at all? That's right, no distributor. Actually, it's more common than many people may think. There are very few, if any, new vehicles with distributors in the engine.

As electronic engine management systems progressed, the roles of the distributor continued to diminish until they completely disappeared! The majority of racing and performance cars are still using distributors, which is why we will be including them throughout this discussion. However, the distributorless contingent is growing. Even so, either ignition system still needs a trigger source and electronics to control the charging and operation of the coils, whether that is through the distributor or through an ECU and electronic ignition module.

There are several variations of the distributorless ignition systems (DIS). There are coil pack models where a coil has two towers and fires two cylinders. There are ignition systems that have a coil for every cylinder. The latest systems even have the coil mounted right to the spark plug so there's not even a plug wire! The DIS coil pack systems have a variety of ignition upgrades available. There are even companies that specialize in an entire system that allows you to obsolete your own distributor. We'll get into more detail on these systems in later chapters. Whatever type of ignition system your engine sports, there are shared traits between all ignitions, including what it takes to upgrade their performance.

at high speeds. They also need to be able to deliver high levels of voltage, while suppressing electromagnetic interference (EMI), which is created when high voltage passes through a wire.

EMI is sometimes known as radio noise. It can not only be an annoying buzz on your radio, but it can also wreak havoc on other electronics within your vehicle such as the rev limiter, or even the ECU of a car equipped with an EFI system. Original equipment spark plug wires combat EMI by using a carbon core material that has a very high resistance to the flow of energy. These will do for stock-performing daily drivers, but when it comes to high-performance ignition systems, a wire with lower resistance and high EMI suppression capability is needed.

Another area of importance in the spark plug wire is the crimp between the terminal and the wire. Poor crimps can contribute to intermittent performance, a dead cylinder, and other problems. Also pay attention to the spark plug wire boots, as they need to survive parked in close proximity to the exhaust manifolds where heat is at its most extreme.

SPARK PLUGS

The final leap that the spark needs to take is across the gap of the spark

Even if your engine doesn't have a distributor, the theory of the ignition system remains common with the original version. Instead of a trigger from the distributor going to the coil, there's a signal from a crankshaft sensor that is responsible for triggering the coil's high voltage.

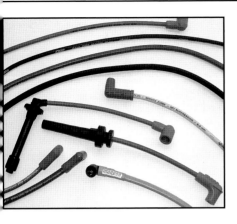

Plug wires play a final role in the ignition system. Wires need to be able to handle nasty underhood temperatures and the high voltage and current that the ignition produces. If a wire fails, you'll feel it for sure.

plug itself. It's the ignition's last hurrah, that is, if everything is planned correctly. The spark transfers from the plug wire terminal to the threaded tip of the plug's center terminal. This terminal reaches all the way through the ceramic shell of the plug and ends at the electrode. From there, there is a gap to the electrode of the plug that is connected to the metal housing of the plug, which forms a ground to the engine. The voltage jumps the gap to the electrode. The resulting spark ignites the air/fuel mixture in the cylinder and ta-da! The ignition cycle starts all over for the next cylinder in the firing order.

You'll find that there are a variety of spark plug and spark plug manufacturers, each with their own theories on why one is better than the other. There are platinum-tipped plugs, plugs with tiny electrodes, some with numerous electrodes, and more. There are also spark plugs called resistor plugs, nonresistor plugs, hot plugs, and cold plugs.

Another area of the spark plug that can affect the engine's performance is the distance of the spark plug gap. Opening the gap forces the coil to build up a higher voltage in order for the spark to jump the gap. However, the plug gap is affected by the engine's compression and cylinder pressures. High cylinder pressure from nitrous or forced induction will place limits on the plug gap. Too large of a gap will also put added pressure on the secondary side of the ignition system, resulting in shortening the life of the components. Too small of a gap can make life too easy on the ignition to the point where the resulting spark may not be strong enough to create a full combustion cycle of the air/fuel mixture.

IGNITION CONTROLS

When you have all of the parts we just went over installed correctly, you'll have an operational ignition system. One of the most popular ways to upgrade an ignition's output is by wiring in an external ignition control. You've probably seen these controls at shows, races, and in the magazines. Plus you'll spend the next two chapters reading about how they work!

If your car is firing on the stock ignition system, adding one of these controls is an easy and effective way to improve performance. Most of these controls wire to the primary side of the ignition and deliver a much hotter spark to the coil. They can also enhance the dwell control, resulting in big spark improvements on the secondary side.

Obviously, a factory ignition system doesn't require an aftermarket ignition control, though many aftermarket distributors do.

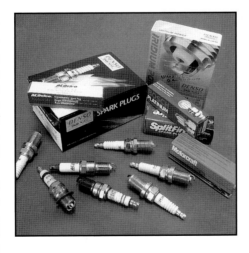

Spark plugs are the final step in the ignition process. As with most of the ignition system, there are a lot of different plugs available, but they all serve the same purpose — to light the fuel mixture!

An aftermarket ignition control can spice up your stock ignition's output. Many different controls are available to cover most any ignition system out there, even distributorless ignition systems.

BATTERY AND CHARGING SYSTEM

Unless your engine uses a magneto, you're going to need a battery to get the engine fired up, and to supply the ignition with current and voltage created by the alternator. The battery is the main source of power for a performance ignition system, and you need to be sure that it's capable of providing the juice that the ignition system requires during heavy-duty operation.

There's more relying on the battery than just the ignition system. The starter is also gulping up huge amounts of current to roll over your street or race engine. Also, any other electrical devices such as fans, pumps, motors, and even fuel injection controls all tap into the battery for voltage.

Alternators are used on all street cars and, any more, even on the majority of race engines. The alternator is responsible for producing the electricity that a car draws out of the battery while it is running. The alternator generates an alternating current (AC) when it is turned by a belt and pulley connected to the crankshaft. With the engine running, a rotor is spun inside the alternator, which creates a magnetic field. This field is induced into the windings of a stator, and eventually makes its way to the battery. If you run a battery without a charging system, it is important that it's fully charged at the beginning of the race so it has the capacity to power all of your car's electrical needs through the finish line.

THE SUM OF THE PARTS

As you can see, the ignition system has several key components and all of them work together to produce a spark and deliver it at the right moment in the engine cycle. Remember, your ignition system is going to be a sum of all of these parts working as a team. If one part isn't up its task, the entire system suffers. If the rotor is worn, the spark isn't going to make it to the plugs. If the coil is shorted out, its spark output is going to suffer. Therefore, it is important that the entire system is kept in check through maintenance and assembled and wired correctly from the start.

There are a variety of ignition systems and components available for your performance car, truck, or whatever you race. Each component has its own pros and perhaps cons, but all components share the same ultimate goal – to create combustion.

So there's a brief overview of the ignition system and what it needs to accomplish millions of times during a race or even just a cruise down to the local burger stand. In the following chapters, we'll explore each of these areas in much more detail. Lets get started!

The battery is imperative to your ignition system's performance, not to mention anything that runs off electricity on your car. Its cohort, the alternator, must be able to meet the charging requirements of your car's electrical system and keep the battery charged.

Component Selection

The ignition, as you'll find out, is an integral part of your car's performance. As you read through these chapters, please note that we try to explain how different components work and the benefits of them. This is not meant to be a catalog for ignition components, and we did not set out to compare or pit one component against another one. If you want to read more about a component's output specs or other features, go to the company's website or get their catalog.

This text is meant to explain the different areas of an automotive ignition and the ways that you can achieve better performance by adding to and tuning your ignition. Once you have a grasp on an ignition's operation, you'll be able to select the parts you need for your engine to perform up to its potential.

IGNITION CONTROLS
An Intro to Performance Ignitions

This book is about building a performance ignition system for your vehicle, whatever your vehicle may be, and that means covering a variety of applications. Luckily, there are a lot of different ignition controls, coils, distributors, and spark plug wires to choose from. This is a good thing for two reasons: For starters, there is plenty of information that you can research in the catalogs, ads, and magazines to find the right parts that will give you the bang, or in this case the spark, for your buck. The second reason is that there's plenty of information to write about for this book!

Just like when you're building a car, you need to have a plan. Even a loose plan will do. We all know that car building plans can change on a whim! If you plan on the engine producing about 350 horsepower, you know you don't need to spend the extra money for a set of race prepped axles, a carbon fiber driveshaft, or an MSD Programmable Digital-7 Ignition Control and crank trigger (you'll read more about those in later chapters). That would just be overkill! Mind you, overkill certainly does have its place in a high-performance car, but not when you're working on a budget. The point here is that if you don't know what you're looking for in an ignition, you can easily be steered into overkill, or even worse, not have enough fire get

your engine going. The ideal ignition system should be somewhere between just right and a little over-the-top.

INDUCTIVE AND CAPACITIVE DISCHARGE IGNITIONS

Automotive ignition systems can be broken down into two distinct groups: inductive discharge and capacitive discharge. An inductive ignition is the most common system, because they're used to fire the majority of stock engines. A factory inductive ignition system gets the job of creating combus-

tion in the cylinder done in an adequate fashion, but there are certainly steps you can take to improve an inductive ignition's output.

An inductive system relies on the coil to come through and carry the brunt of the system's work. The coil is responsible for taking in battery voltage (12 – 14 volts) and stepping it up to thousands of volts to create a spark that is capable of jumping the gap of the spark plug to ignite the air/fuel mixture. To accomplish this feat, the coil is made up of two series of windings, the primary and secondary, along with an iron

There are a lot of different things to consider when you're selecting an ignition control for your engine. Would your engine benefit from a capacitive discharge ignition? Would a rev limiter be a good idea, or is the ignition compatible with your existing distributor? The answers lie ahead.

core to strengthen the magnetic field that is created as the battery current flows through the primary windings.

The primary windings are usually several hundred turns of a heavier wire, while the secondary windings are a finer wire with several thousand windings. (This gives you the turns ratio that you see in coil specifications, which will be covered in detail in Chapter 4.) When the switching device opens, whether it is breaker points or an electronic trigger source, it causes the current flow through the primary windings to stop, which forces the magnetic field to collapse across to the secondary windings. This induces a very high voltage that is sent out of the coil through the secondary side of the ignition (out of the spark plug terminal) to the distributor. To summarize, the coil must take in the supply voltage, store it, and step it up to a high voltage every time it is signaled to do so. It then releases whatever high voltage is needed to jump the spark plug gap. That's quite a workload.

Like most systems that are used by the factory, the inductive ignition system gets the job done, but is adequate at best. Even when it comes to OEM standards, the stock ignition systems are limited (okay, the past few years the factory has done a much better job). But that's the way OEMs need things: inexpensive to mass produce, yet reliable

and able to perform well enough to get the average Joe down the road and back home. If you're reading this book, you are probably not Joe Average, since you are looking for a way to get a hotter spark out of your ignition.

The biggest downfall or hurdle of the inductive ignition design is the storage and build-up of the voltage. It takes a certain amount of time, called dwell, for the coil to transform the lower battery voltage to the higher voltage required to jump the spark plug gap. This works just fine at lower RPM, but what happens as RPM increases? There may not be enough time for the coil to step up the battery voltage in between firings. This can result in a low voltage spark output that may not be powerful enough to light the air/fuel mixture in the cylinder. This can result in a misfire and loss of power.

Using a physical analogy is probably easier than trying to picture all of this electrical stuff happening. Think about using a faucet to fill a bucket with water. Once the bucket is topped off, you pour it into a big barrel. What happens if you need to start emptying the bucket faster and faster? If the pressure and volume of water coming out of the faucet doesn't increase, the buckets

This is the capacitor of an MSD 6 Series Ignition. Next to it is the transformer that receives power directly from the battery and steps it up to nearly 500 volts. The capacitor stores this voltage until the ignition is triggered, at which point all of the voltage is delivered to the coil.

aren't going to be filled to the top when you pour them in the barrel. The same falls true of an inductive ignition system. Their main downfall is at higher RPM, when they cannot meet the quicker rise time of the voltage that's required of them.

There are inductive ignition controls that will improve the performance of your stock ignition system through improved control of the coil charge time and supply voltage. The MSD Blaster Ignition is a compact and economically priced inductive control.

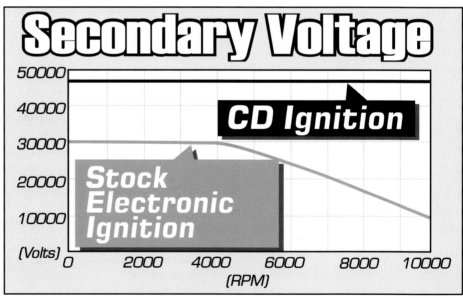

This graph illustrates the difference between the secondary voltage of an inductive ignition and a capacitive discharge ignition control. As RPM increases, the inductive output will eventually fall due to the lack of time between firings. The CD ignition is always at full output power.

That isn't to say that distributor triggered inductive ignition systems don't have their place in the performance world. In fact, with advances in high-current circuit controls and digital monitors, you may see more high-output inductive ignitions in the not so distant future. Today, inductive ignitions serve their purpose well in many applications. They can be very cost effective and are capable of producing a long duration spark, which is a benefit in the combustion chamber. The aftermarket has done a good job producing performance based inductive ignition components; we'll get to that soon. In fact, there are a couple unique systems designed to take advantage of an inductive ignition's positive characteristics. Before we get deeper into these offerings, we'll go over a brief introduction to the capacitive discharge ignition.

CAPACITIVE DISCHARGE

Capacitive discharge (CD) designed ignition controls have been the mainstay of performance ignition systems since the mid 1970s. Their biggest advantage is their ability to produce full-power sparks throughout the engine's entire RPM range with no fear of a weak spark at the top end. This is because a CD ignition draws its voltage supply directly from the battery and uses a custom wound transformer to step up this voltage to close to 500 volts and higher. This voltage is stored at full strength and is at the ready in the ignition's capacitor. Once the ignition receives a trigger signal, all of this voltage is dumped into the coil where it is stepped up to the high voltage that is required at the spark plug gap. Depending on which coil is being used, the voltage could reach up to and over 30,000 – 45,000 volts!

A capacitive discharge ignition delivers the high voltage to the spark plug that is required to ionize, or create a bridge across the plug gap in order for the spark energy to flow across. The downfall that may come with a CD ignition is that the spark has a very short duration. At lower RPM, this could present a problem, but engineers

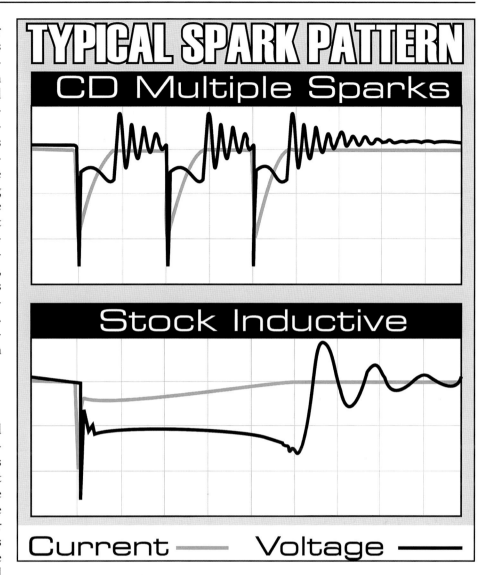

This chart illustrates the multi-sparking capabilities of most capacitive discharge ignition controls. Each spark is at full output power and the series of sparks generally lasts for 20° of crankshaft rotation.

found a solution by firing the plug multiple times in the same cycle. Hence, the multiple spark discharge, multi-strike, or second strike terms you read about in ads and catalogs. Most CD ignitions create multiple sparks when the engine is below 3,000 – 3,300 rpm. The number of sparks that occur increases as the RPM drops, because there is more time to fire the plug. At an idle there may be five or six sparks, but there may only be two at 2,700 rpm. Even with its shorter duration, a single CD spark has no trouble igniting the air/fuel mixture at engine speeds over 3,300 rpm.

A lot of people look at CD ignitions as race-only pieces, but that is not the case. In fact, a lot of these ignitions are legal to install on pollution-controlled engines – and some are even legal to install on OBD equipped cars. Most ignition controls are nearly universal in their application, as these can be installed on most anything with a distributor. Finding a newer car with a distributor is getting tough, so there are also ignitions available for these distributorless systems as well. These will be discussed in later chapters as well.

The series of full-power sparks that most CD ignitions produce creates more heat in the cylinder, resulting in improved combustion of the air/fuel mixture. In most cases, the benefits

Stack It Up

What if you were to combine an inductive ignition with a CD ignition? Wouldn't that give you the best of both worlds, since there are benefits to each of these spark profiles? Inductive ignitions have a long spark duration, yet their initial voltage output suffers at higher RPM. Capacitive discharge systems have terrific initial voltage to deal with high combustion-chamber pressures, but they use it all up and do not offer a long duration.

There are a couple products that have been recently introduced that combine the best of these two ignition designs. MSD's Stacker Ignition connects to your stock ignition inductive system and delivers a high-power CD spark or even multiple sparks, on top of the factory inductive spark. The benefits are gained from the full power spark at higher RPM where the factory ignition falters and even at idle and low RPM, thanks to multiple sparks.

Pertronix also offers an ignition that provides two sparks in one, called

The MSD Stacker Ignition wires inline with your car's stock ignition system and delivers a CD spark 'stacked' on top of the factory inductive spark. This gives you the best of both spark profiles. MSD offers a Stacker unit for engines with distributors and also for distributorless systems.

the Second Strike. Their unit allows you to choose when the CD spark occurs in the cylinder by adjusting a rotary dial. This can help you dial-in the ignition to match your application.

Chrysler has offered performance ignition modules for their electronic ignition systems almost since they switched from points. Their Orange box is good through 6,000 rpm, the Chrome box is rated through 8,000 rpm, and the Super Gold is designed for race-only applications.

miles or poorly tuned carb, some extra spark energy will help.

Most of the add-on inductive ignition controls simply do a better job of controlling the high current and dwell time of the primary supply voltage. The technology wasn't available to the OEMs when they first started doing electronic ignitions, or it simply wasn't economical for them to manufacture. Remember, only a fraction of people driving want to make sure their engine has no problem pulling steady through 6,000 rpm! Knowing that, it's still strange how many of the OEM's now offer components and kits to up the fire power of their own ignition systems! Ford even offers an "Extra Performance Ignition" for their electronic Duraspark ignitions used in 1976 through the mid 1980s. This system features improved spark output and even has an adjustable rev limiter. This system is used to replace Ford modules that have a blue or yellow wire strain relief. If your Ford is equipped with a Duraspark system, take a look at where the wires come out of the box. There will be a plastic strain relief and it should be blue or yellow. If not, don't try the Extra Performance Module as damage to the ignition system may occur.

include an improved idle, quick starts, crisp throttle response, and improved high-RPM performance. If you have an engine that burns a little oil, runs a touch on the rich side, or the like, a multiple sparking ignition, CD or inductive, could help overcome these troubles. That is, until they can be remedied correctly.

It's interesting to note that adding more primary voltage to the coil is key in producing increased secondary voltage to get to the spark plug. A CD ignition delivers hundreds of volts into the coil so thousands more get produced in the coil resulting in a crisp spark at the plug gap. An inductive ignition requires a good power source, as do all ignitions, but most of the add-on ignition controls that are inductive are designed to improve the control of the primary voltage through advanced dwell control

and storage. There are quite a few controls available. Even though most performance enthusiasts cut right to CD ignitions, there are still a lot of inductive ignition offerings.

INDUCTIVE ADD-ONS

There are several options if you want to add a little extra oomph to your ignition system but prefer to maintain the original distributor and coil to keep things as simple as possible. Most of the aftermarket performance ignition companies produce economically priced ignition components that will add a little more zing to an inductive ignition. When you add a little extra spark to the ignition, you'll generally see an improvement in the way the car starts and idles. If your engine takes a while to fire up or runs a bit rough due to high

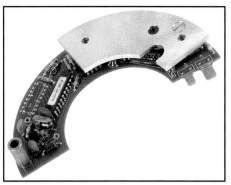

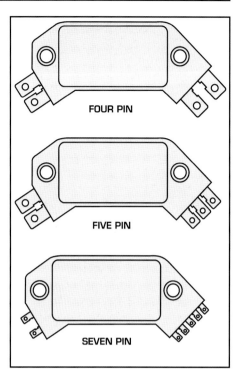

If you simply want to give your breaker points system a little kick, the Mallory Hyfire I is easy to wire and increases the primary voltage to the coil, resulting in higher secondary voltage. The amount of time that the spark burns across the gap is also increased.

There are a variety of ignition modules available to add some zing to a GM HEI distributor. Mallory's new design offers increased output with improved timing control, plus it has a rev limiter built into the board that is adjustable from 4,000 – 5,800 rpm.

This chart shows the visual difference between GM HEI modules throughout the years. The 4-pin module is from the first generation of HEI modules and is the model that most aftermarket companies offer performance replacement modules for. The 5- and 7-pin modules incorporated only minor timing control operation that limits their use in the performance realm.

Crane offers an inductive Multi-Spark Ignition that easily connects to points, amplifiers, or other electronic triggers. Below 2,500 rpm, Crane's Fast Inductive Restrike technology produces a long duration spark then quickly recharges the coil and fires the same plug again.

MSD, though known for multiple sparking CD ignitions, also offers a couple inductive controls. Their Blaster Ignition Control produces a powerful single spark with lengthy spark duration. This compact unit is easy to wire and delivers a much hotter spark to the coil. For an old cruiser with points, this is an economical way to improve the ignition's output and the engine's performance. MSD also offers an MSD 5 Ignition, which seems to be somewhat of the red headed stepchild of their ignitions. The MSD 5 is an inductive ignition, but it still manages to produce multiple sparks at

lower RPM. The difference is that the sparks may not have full power every time like their CD systems.

GM's HEI Distributor

In the early 1970s when General Motors developed their electronic High Energy Ignition (HEI) distributor, they probably didn't think that they'd still be using them in the 21st century! No, the HEI is not in any of their new cars rolling off the line, but they are still bolting them in place on many of their performance crate engines.

This distributor is unique in that its construction is entirely unitized. That is, there is only one wire to connect, and the coil is incorporated into the distributor cap. This feature has made this inductive distributor a favorite among performance enthusiasts and is even mandated in some racing sanctions. But like most OEM components, the HEI distributor was built for average applications and average drivers, so it suffers at higher RPM, just like most other inductive ignitions. Since these distributors are so popular in the performance world there are easy ways to bulk up their performance.

The HEI uses an electronic trigger, so there is an ignition module that controls the flow and charge time of the voltage. Of course, throughout the years, there were changes made to the

ignition module, so you first need to identify the module by counting its number of terminals. There were three modules used. The first, and most popular module had four terminals, and these distributors area easy to spot because they still used a vacuum advance. Next came the short-lived use of a 5-pin module. These were only used for a limited time before the 7-pin module came into play. These two later modules had electronic timing curves built into them. The 7-pin was even used with an engine knock sensor and had electronic timing control built into it. The obvious choice for performance use is the older 4-pin distributors, and this is the one that is available from many ignition companies. It is usually identified by having a vacuum advance canister, though a few of these may have the 5-pin module.

Reading Between the Lines

There are many racing sanctions, mostly circle track racing, that mandate in their rulebooks the use of an HEI distributor. Some leave it at that, while others attach comments that it must be a stock appearing HEI distributor. This leaves a little gray area for racers to ponder. Does stock appearing mean it must look stock from the outside? Or does that mean the module and coil must appear stock looking as well? Some of the HEI Modules offered from Mallory or MSD do not have a stock appearance, so which way of thinking is

right? That's up to your tech department to decide, so before you try upgrading your distributor for racing, you better check to see what they consider is legal or "stock appearing."

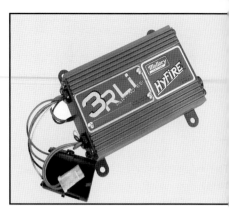

The Mallory Hyfire 3RLi Ignition Control increases the primary energy and voltage to the coil. It also optimizes the dwell through higher RPM and produces a stronger spark. This control also has one rev limiter for over-rev protection and one for staging control.

The Davis Unified Distributors from Performance Distributors can be made to look factory stock but will pack a powerful punch. This of course won't get by tech in a Chrysler or Ford, since they were never offered as original equipment on these engines!

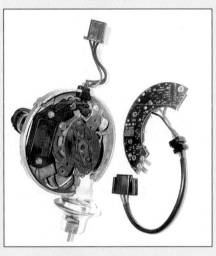

The MSD HEI module probably won't pass as stock appearing when compared side-by-side to a stock version.

The HPX distributorless Electromotive ignition is an inductive system that uses multiple coil packs. Since each coil only fires twice throughout an engine's complete firing cycle, there is much more time for each coil to charge to full capacity.

Installing an inductive ignition control to an HEI can almost be considered redundant. The HEI already is an electronic inductive ignition, albeit one that could use a boost. Going with an aftermarket module and coil are the best ways to boost the output of your HEI. One thing to check before you add components to your HEI is to make sure that it will be receiving a solid 12 – 14 volts and that the supply wire is at least 14 gauge. The system can't produce high voltage if it doesn't have enough power supply to work with!

AND NOW FOR SOMETHING COMPLETELY DIFFERENT

With all apologies to Monty Python's Flying Circus, we just couldn't resist, nor could we think of a more apt header to introduce the Electromotive Ignition System. Electromotive is an inductive ignition system that does not use a distributor. Rather than a single coil and distributor, the Electromotive system uses multiple dual-tower coil packs to deliver a powerful, long-duration spark to the plugs.

Capacitive discharge ignitions are not the only high-performance ignition system used. Electromotive takes advantage of an inductive ignition's long spark duration. By incorporating one coil for every two cylinders, each coil has plenty of time to charge to full capacity. In fact, the time available to recharge each coil goes up four times on an 8-cylinder engine since it does not have to fire every spark plug.

We will get more involved with distributorless ignition systems and Electromotive's offerings in later chapters, but wanted to include their unique (and patented) inductive system while talking about inductive systems and street/strip ignition controls.

The Crane Import Power HI-6S ignition control is a compact ignition control that is designed for tuner performance. The advanced inductive circuits help extend the spark duration to improve combustion and performance of smaller displacement engines.

AFTERMARKET CAPACITIVE DISCHARGE IGNITIONS

The thing to note about most of the CD ignition controls available is that they aren't too much more of an investment over an inductive control. Plus they offer a lot of great driveability benefits and will accept ignition accessory upgrades over the long haul. Keep in mind that multiple sparking CD ignitions are not just for high-performance race cars! In fact, most of the units we're going to discuss in this chapter even carry CARB approval numbers, meaning that they're legal to install on vehicles in all 50 states. Mind you, this depends on the year of the vehicle and the model of ignition that you choose. The point is that by achieving better combustion resulting from high-power and multiple sparks, an ignition control can benefit everything from your daily grocery getter to a weekend bracket racer.

The street version of a multiple sparking CD ignition begins with the 6 Series Ignition Controls. All of the companies kind of kept things simple by using the same number series to denote the performance level of their different ignition controls (to an extent). Most any engine that is equipped with a distributor and a 12-volt, negative-ground electrical system can accept a CD ignition. There are a few, very few, import vehicles out there that actually had CD systems installed from the factory, and these will not

There are many entry-level CD ignition controls to choose from, such as Crane's HI-6. All of these ignitions produce multiple sparks and deliver a high primary voltage to the coil for improved spark output. Some of the benefits of a CD ignition are improved throttle response, top-end performance, idle, and starting.

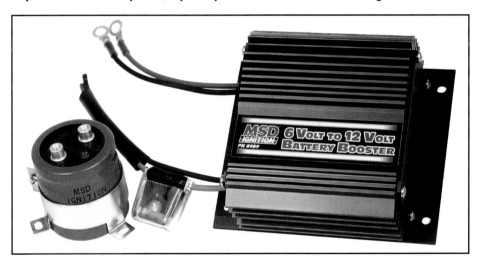

CD ignition controls all require a 12-volt negative-ground electrical system, which leaves a lot of classics and imports out in the cold. MSD offers this 6-to-12 Volt Booster that will wire into negative-ground, six-volt systems and supply the ignition control with 12 volts. That way you can install a multiple sparking ignition control.

accept an aftermarket CD system. Except a handful of examples, most everything out there from 4, 6, or 8-cylinder engines are candidates for improved spark power.

Notice that we mentioned the need for a distributor with these ignition controls. In recent years, distributorless ignition systems (DIS) have pretty much replaced the distributor. First

came coil packs with two or more towers, then with individual coils for each cylinder, and now there are even coil-on-plug systems coming from the factories. DIS systems were used in the mid 1980s, for example, the turbocharged, intercooled Buick Grand Nationals were fitted with a dual-tower coil-pack assembly. The aftermarket companies are working with these DIS systems,

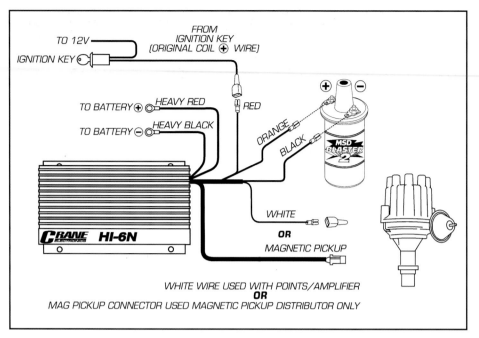

TO 12V

IGNITION KEY

FROM IGNITION KEY (ORIGINAL COIL ⊕ WIRE)

TO BATTERY ⊕ — HEAVY RED

TO BATTERY ⊖ — HEAVY BLACK

RED

ORANGE

BLACK

MSD BLASTER 2

CRANE HI-6N

WHITE
OR
MAGNETIC PICKUP

WHITE WIRE USED WITH POINTS/AMPLIFIER
OR
MAG PICKUP CONNECTOR USED MAGNETIC PICKUP DISTRIBUTOR ONLY

This diagram shows how easy it is to wire in a CD ignition control. There's really only four wires to connect, plus the battery supply wires. Remember, these can be installed on most any engine equipped with a distributor and a 12-volt negative-ground system.

and most of them have multi-channel controls available for the systems with multiple coil packs. We'll get into these DIS components more in later chapters. For now, we're sticking with ignition systems that incorporate a distributor.

As long as there's a distributor and a single coil, such as on a 1.8-liter Honda, an inline 6-cylinder truck, or an LT-1 Camaro with the distributor mounted behind the water pump, an ignition control can be added. Most ignition controls are quite universal, and if you can get to the trigger wire(s) and the coil terminals, you can do it. A CD ignition control will have two power source wires that supply the battery voltage and ground, one wire to turn the unit on and off, a coil positive wire, a coil negative wire, and a trigger input wire. Usually, there is a trigger input that accepts a signal from points or an amplifier and another connector that has two wires for a magnetic pickup. You'll either use the points wire or the magnetic pickup wires, but never both at the same time.

It's also important to note that when you connect the primary coil wires, these are the only wires that will be connected to the coil termi-

nals. Don't try to connect your tach to the coil's negative terminal any longer, because once the CD ignition is in place, there will be up to 500 volts on the coil's primary side. Also, be sure not to connect any test equipment such as test lights or dwell meters to the coil anymore. Damage to your testers and to yourself could occur! If you have an aftermarket tachometer that was connected to the negative terminal of the coil, don't hook it back up! All of the CD ignitions will have a tach output terminal that will produce a common 12-volt square wave signal that should trigger the tach. On certain, shall we say, low-cost bargain-type tachs, there may be some troubles. Again, this generally should not give you a problem, but if your tach has trouble reading the CD ignition's tach signal, you may need a tach adapter, available from the ignition manufacturer, to fix the problem. (See the sidebar on tach adaptors.)

What's Available?

The most popular street/strip capacitive discharge ignitions are the 6A and the 6AL from MSD. The only difference between the two is that the 6AL has a built-in rev control (note the "L" for limiter). With this being recognized as a good entry-level ignition, Mallory

One of the most recent introductions into the capacitive discharge arena is from Fire Control/Jacobs ignition systems, which is now a member of the Mr. Gasket group. Their FC 3000 Ignition is digitally controlled and has a built-in rev limiter.

Tach or Stalling Troubles?

With as many applications there are in the automotive world, you are bound to run into a couple cars or engines that will trip you and the ignition companies up. For instance, after installing a CD ignition on your Toyota, it will start and run rough, then stall. Or maybe the tachometer on your 5.0-liter Mustang reads erratically.

Chances are that most of these ignition companies have run into the problem you're experiencing and they know how to fix it. The most common fix is with what they call tach adapters, even though they'll do more than simply fix the tachometer. Most of these adapters easily wire into the system and modify the trigger signal by making it stronger, so it can feed both the ignition and the ECU to trigger the fuel injection. Other models can be used to work with current triggered tachometers.

Tach adapters aren't required on the majority of installations, but there are a handful that will require one, such as most Toyotas.

The Crane Tach Adapter may be needed on some magnetic triggered applications on pre-1981 cars and pre-1986 trucks without computers. It will also work to deliver a trigger signal to current triggered tachs that were available on some older cars.

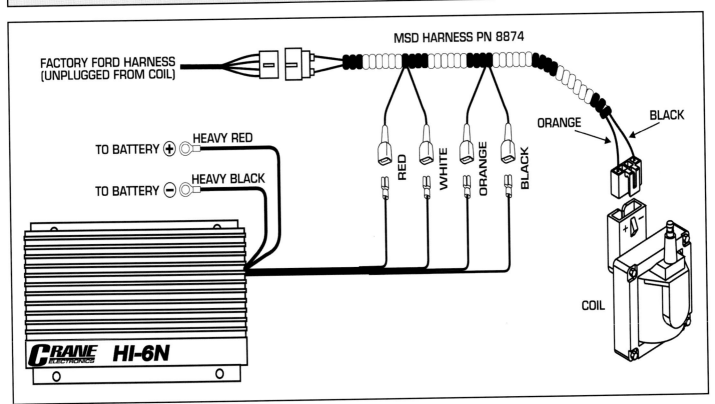

With late-model EFI comes more intimidating wiring. But fear not, most of the ignition companies offer handy harnesses for popular applications. These make installing one of their ignitions a breeze, with no cutting or splicing. This diagram shows a Crane HI-6 wired to a 5.0-liter TFI Ford with a matching harness.

The Points to Using a CD Ignition

There are a variety of electronic conversions for factory-style distributors with breaker points, but there are also other options. As long as the distributor is in good mechanical condition, why not install a CD ignition to the system? Think about it, not only would you receive the benefits of the ignition's multiple sparks and high voltage, but the points will last much longer and won't require much (if any) maintenance.

A CD ignition won't cost too much more than the replacement kits available and if you don't mind mounting the control box and dealing with a few more wires, the benefits are twofold. When a CD ignition, such as a 6-Series model, is wired to a points system, the points are only responsible for triggering the ignition. The transformer in the ignition steps up the voltage and stores

it in its own capacitor. When the points trigger the box, all of this voltage is delivered directly to the coil, where the voltage is stepped up even further and sent to the spark plugs.

So you can see the performance improvements, but another benefit is that the points will last much longer. Originally, when the points open, there will be 3-4 amps of current going across their gap. This is the main cause of the points to wear. With the CD ignition installed, the breaker points are used only to trigger the unit when to fire so there's less than three tenths of an amp bridging the gap!

If looking to keep up a stock appearance and don't want to deal with mounting and wiring an ignition control box, the points replacement kits will be covered in Chapter 5.

The Mallory line of 6-Series ignitions includes a Digital Hyfire VI-A and VI-AL. These are both microprocessor-controlled ignitions that easily connect to points, amplifiers, and magnetic pickup distributors. Like the other CD ignitions, they can be used on 4-, 6-, or 8-cylinder engines.

processor watching over everything. MSD does offer a line of digitally controlled ignitions, which we'll get into more later on.

Crane Cams came into the performance ignition market with their line of Fireball digitally controlled ignition systems nearly 10 years ago. Their street CD system is called the HI-6 and they have several versions with different options and accessories available. This base unit offers a built-in rev limiter that is adjusted with rotary dials, so there is no need for extra RPM modules. Like the other CD ignitions shown here, the HI-6 produces a series of full power multiple sparks that last for 20° crankshaft rotation through about 3,000 rpm. Another nifty feature it offers is an LED that will flash trouble codes if there are any problems with the installation.

The CD ignition controls from Fire Control, such as their FC 3000 ignition, feature a dual-stage output system. At moderate RPM, the ignition knows that a full power spark is not required, so the ignition knows to step back its output. But when it senses an increase in RPM, it kicks back in to full spark output. This feature is unique to Fire Control and is designed to help preserve the life of the secondary ignition components, as well as the operation of the battery and charging system.

Mallory, one of the original per-

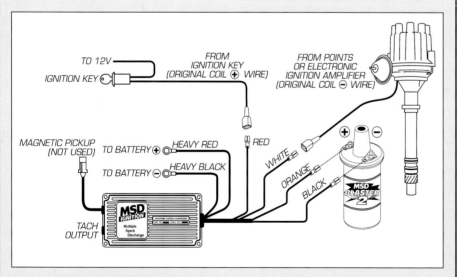

This is how easy it is to connect an MSD 6A or similar CD ignition control to a distributor with points. Benefits include better performance (due to the higher voltage sparks), longer points life, and a back-up ignition. If you were to ever experience problems with the ignition, you can easily bypass it and use the points to get home!

and Crane both stuck with the 6-Series tag, which makes things easier for everyone involved. The MSD 6AL is an analog controlled ignition. This essen-

tially means that its operation is controlled through a variety of resistors, transistors, diodes, and other electronic components. In short, there's no micro-

It Runs Great — But It Keeps Running!

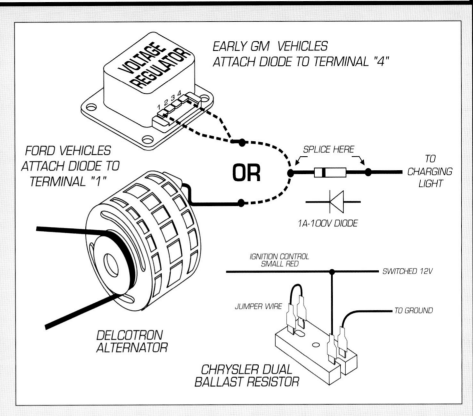

VOLTAGE REGULATOR

EARLY GM VEHICLES
ATTACH DIODE TO TERMINAL "4"

FORD VEHICLES
ATTACH DIODE TO
TERMINAL "1"

OR

SPLICE HERE

TO CHARGING LIGHT

1A-100V DIODE

DELCOTRON ALTERNATOR

IGNITION CONTROL
SMALL RED

SWITCHED 12V

JUMPER WIRE

TO GROUND

CHRYSLER DUAL
BALLAST RESISTOR

You just wired in a multiple sparking CD ignition in your '65 Chevelle and give the key a twist to hear the 327 fire up quicker than it ever has. "All right," you think as you move back under the hood, "this ignition does make a difference!" You snap the throttle a couple times and notice a difference in how quick the engine responds. A smile comes over your face and the satisfying feeling that your time and money were well spent. A cruise will be the final test, but first to clean up a little. You lean in the window to turn the key off — but the engine continues purring along. "What the....?"

This can happen on a few older vehicles, especially ones with external voltage regulators. What is occurring is that the small wire that is responsible for turning the ignition control on and off is connected to a wire that is receiving a feedback, most likely from the charging system dash indicator bulb. This can make just enough voltage to keep the ignition running even though the key is turned off. In most cases, this is an easy fix with a diode that is often supplied with many of the CD ignitions. This diode will keep the current flowing in one direction so it cannot feedback.

The diagrams show where to install it on several different applications. This may not be the fix for a few AMC engines. For these, using a Chrysler Dual Ballast Resistor, as shown in the diagram, will fix the no-stop troubles.

This diagram shows which wire a diode would need to be installed on to prevent the engine from not shutting off. A dual-ballast resistor is also shown for Chrysler/AMC applications.

formance ignition companies, recently developed a nicely priced CD ignition called the Hyfire VI-A. This ignition is digitally controlled and produces a stout series of high-voltage sparks at any RPM. Mallory also followed with a Hyfire VI-AL, which, like the MSD version, is equipped with a built-in rev limiter. This version is adjustable with rotary dials rather than the plug-in modules that MSD uses. This does make changes easier.

Digital and Analog Ignition Controls

So what's the big buzz on digitally controlled ignition controls? The big deal is that the ignition utilizes a micro-controller to manage the RPM limits and review the trigger signals and functions of the ignition. Like most things that incorporate digital controllers, these ignitions can be more efficient in the way they manage the voltage and trigger signals resulting in improved accuracy. Plus many of them can have more features such as rev limiters and timing controls built into a small housing.

Does this mean that analog controls are on the way out? Not entirely. Crane, MSD, Mallory, and Fire Control all still have analog controlled ignitions. These analog ignitions are used with great success and from the number of ignitions you see out there, that

becomes pretty obvious. In fact, most of the power-making components within a digital ignition use analog circuitry. But there is no denying digitally controlled ignitions and technology, especially when it seems like most anything new that comes out is digitally controlled in some manner! If your application doesn't need a two-step rev control, retard stage, or other features, you might be able to save a few bucks by going with a no frills analog ignition.

This just scratches the clear coat in the world of performance ignition controls. The next chapter will lead us into CD controls that offer more options and more power – much more power!

CD IGNITION CONTROLS
High-Performance Racing Ignitions

The Fire Control FC 4000 is a digital CD ignition and offers a two-step rev limiter that is adjusted with rotary dials. Fire Control incorporates what they call acceleration spark technology. At moderate throttle, the box's output is lowered to reduce heat and excessive wear on the secondary components. When there is an increase in RPM, the spark output returns to full power

Now that you have an understanding on how a capacitive discharge (CD) ignition control works, we'll get into the different models offered and their stages of use. There are a lot of different ignition controls available with a variety of letters and numbers to designate their use or application. In general, they all operate on the same principle, with a transformer to step up the supply voltage and a capacitor to store this high voltage. In fact, most of them wire the same way, just with different color wires.

The ignition is one area where going a little overkill is not going to have too much of an adverse effect on your engine's performance, like too much cam lift or an oversized carburetor would. In most cases, the engine is not going to require the full potential of the ignition's output capabilities! That is, whatever voltage it takes to jump the plug gap is all the ignition is going to need to produce. At moderate throttle, even on a mild street engine, that could be under 20,000 volts (or even less at times). But conversely, much more could be required of the ignition under wide-open throttle romps. So it is good to know that your ignition system is capable of coming through when the demand is there.

This is not to say that you need a Dual Coil MSD 8 racing ignition on your street car. Now that would be overkill. Not only would the spark energy be excessive, but it would also wear the secondary side of the ignition quickly. Not to mention the amount of current an ignition of this magnitude would gulp away from the battery. Besides, these ignitions aren't designed to be driven long distances. This is an extreme example of what it would take to go overkill on an ignition system.

Most of the 6-Series ignition controls will cover applications from cars that are used mostly on the street, to ones that see road course and mild strip duty. The Winston Cup cars are regulated to run analog 6-Series ignition controls and they run for 500 miles at screaming RPM, even with pretty stout compression ratios at times. This kind of use illustrates what these 6-Series controls can live up to.

As we progress up the performance chain of command, there will also be ignition controls that offer common race accessories built into them. This is one of the benefits of microprocessor controls, as they can offer more accessories in a compact package. For this stage of our discussion, we'll limit these accessories to rev limiters and boost or timing retard controls. More timing accessories and adjustments will be introduced in later chapters.

REV LIMITERS

As you invest more time, effort, and money into your engine, you may start to realize the importance of a rev limiter. In the previous chapter we mentioned rev limiters several times, but we didn't go into too much explanation. Since we're continuing into higher-performance systems, the majority of which are offered with one, two, or even three rev limiters, it is something we need to explain.

A rev limiter is made up of a circuit that 'watches' the RPM of the engine. You get to set the limit for your engine (though there are some racing sanctions that impose a rev limit) with an RPM module or through a switch on the ignition. When the engine reaches this RPM, the rev limiting circuits will drop the sparks to different cylinders in order to hold the RPM at the given limit. Even if the throttle is wide open, the goal of the rev limiter is to never let the engine exceed the set RPM point.

This sounds like it would be a fairly simple circuit in the ignition, but a rev limiter has to be ready to handle different over-rev situations. First consider accelerating at a moderate rate. As the engine approaches the rev limit, lets say 7,000 rpm for example, the rev limiting circuit senses the limit and drops the sparks to several cylinders and easily maintains the imposed limit. But what about on a race car that snaps the driveshaft? In this case, the RPM is ramping up at a rapid pace already, but all of a sudden there's little to no load, and zing! Hello rev limiter (and thank you rev limiter). Consider the inertia of the crankshaft or flywheel and the different rates of acceleration that occur in different engines. A rev limiter needs to be able to catch the engine at the determined RPM in order to be accurate and useful to racers.

There are two different kinds of rev limiters that you will hear and read about in catalogs and ads. There is a random limiter, which drops the sparks to various cylinders in no particular order, and a sequential rev limiter. The sequential rev limiter has a pattern or counts the cylinders that it drops the spark out of and makes sure to fire them on the next engine cycle. This is meant to balance the cylinders and keep them from loading up with fuel. Actually, both limiting circuits seem to work well in their own way, and the companies that produce them know how to make each one work well. With better technology for both the analog ignition circuits and especially on the digital side of things, rev limiters seem

These are the infamous chips that you hear about when it comes to changing RPM limits. Inside each module is a different resistor that determines the RPM limit. They're available in 100-rpm increments from 3,000 – 12,000 rpm. This is MSD's SCI-L Ignition that is geared towards the sport compact market.

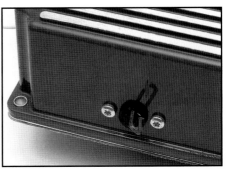

Most rev limiters are set up for use on 8-cylinder engines from the factory. If you're wiring a limiter to a 4- or 6-cylinder engine, be sure to set it up for the correct number of cylinders, or the rev limit will be way off. An MSD 6AL has these wire loops that you need to modify. For even-fire six cylinder engines, cut the red loop. For four-cylinder engines, cut both the red and blue wire loops.

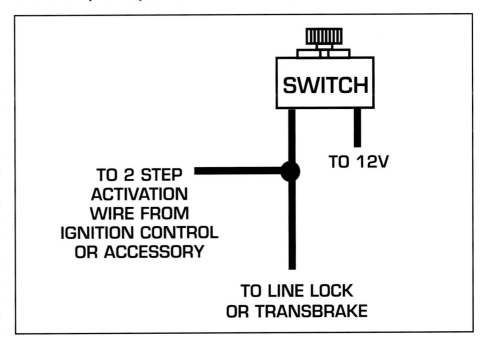

Wiring a two-step rev limit is easy. Generally there is an activation wire that needs to be connected to 12 volts. By connecting it to your line-lock solenoid, or even a hand-held switch, you can activate a lower RPM limit to improve your car's holeshot and your reaction time.

to be getting even smoother while maintaining greater accuracy.

Two Rev Limits

To share the thinking of most racers, if one is good, two must be better. What that line of thinking pertains to here is a dual-stage rev limiter, commonly referred to as a two-step. You'll start hearing about these more as we get into higher-performance ignition controls, especially within the digital control ranks. What a two-step rev limiter offers you is just that, the ability to have two different RPM limits that can be activated independently.

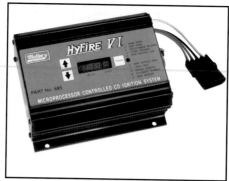

If you have an ignition with a single-stage rev limiter that is adjusted with plug-in modules such as an MSD 6AL or Fire Control FC 2000 ignition, you won't have to buy a new ignition to receive a two-step. Both companies offer add-on Step Module Selectors to provide a high and low RPM limit.

No RPM modules or rotary dials are needed to set the rev limits of the HyFire VI from Mallory. This ignition features an LED screen that lets you scroll through the RPM limits and other optional settings.

Another useful option on a street/strip ignition is a step retard. MSD's Digital SCI+ ignition will provide an adjustable retard that is perfect when nitrous is being introduced to the combustion chamber. The amount of retard is adjusted by these rotary dials next to the two-step adjustment.

The idea behind a two-step is primarily a drag racing accessory, as one limit can be set lower and activated on the starting line. This way, you can put the pedal to the floor and the RPM won't go beyond your set limit. Most of the time, the step RPM limit has an activation wire that you can connect to the line lock or a trans-brake solenoid or other component that you use in the staging lights. Then when the green light comes on, the switch is deactivated and the car launches hard out of the lights. Once the step limit is deactivated, the over-rev limit is in effect and will protect the engine from over-rev damage. A two-step rev limit is handy in helping the car launch consistently, and it lets you concentrate on the Christmas-tree lights rather than the engine RPM.

Street and Strip

Most of the ignitions that feature a two-step rev control are digital models, and they're ideal for cars that see double-duty on the street and strip. You get an engine protecting over-rev limit, plus the consistency that a holeshot rev limit can deliver. The Mallory HyFire VI provides a built-in two-step rev limiter that is easy to adjust by scrolling through the digital display that is installed on top of the housing of the ignition. There are also other adjustable

Crane's HI-6DSR ignition features an over-rev RPM limit as well as a staging RPM limit. Both limits are adjusted with a pair of rotary dials; one sets the thousands and the other dial adjusts in 100-rpm increments for a range from 2,000 – 9,900 rpm.

features built into this ignition that make it ideal for many cars that see duty on the street and the strip.

Other ignitions that share a built-in two-step feature include the MSD Digital-6+, the Fireball HI-6DSR, and Fire Control's new FC 4000. All these digitally controlled units use rotary dials to adjust each of the RPM limits in 100-rpm increments. All of these ignitions are designed to put out a stout amount of voltage with plenty of current. This combination makes them ideal for cars that cruise the streets during the week but are ready to rock at the local digs on the weekend.

MSD's Digital-6+ and their Digital SCI+ Ignition Controls give you the opportunity to set a staging/holeshot rev limiter, plus they have a step retard

option. Retard steps are common accessory in performance ignitions. This is largely due to the popularity of nitrous oxide injection systems. Whenever nitrous is introduced to an engine, the timing should be retarded, because cylinder pressures are going to go up, sometimes way up, depending on how much nitrous is introduced. We'll get more detailed about retard controls and nitrous systems in later chapters, but for now it is important to know that if you plan on running a shot of nitrous on your street/strip car, a step retard is an important feature to have in the ignition system you choose.

Just like the staging RPM rev limit, the step feature has an activation wire that will retard the timing when it is connected to a 12-volt lead. The perfect place to tie this in is by splicing it right into the nitrous solenoid wiring. That way, whenever the nitrous is activated, the timing retard is too. Other ignitions including the Hyfire VI have this feature as well.

Did you notice that all of these ignition controls are digitally controlled? Having a microprocessor watching over the functions of the ignition make it easier to give the user more adjustments and accessories to play with. It seems that the technology for

Keeping Controls Analog

There is absolutely nothing stock about stock car racing. Every car being raced in the NASCAR ranks rolls out of the factory through the power of its front wheels. Not to mention that this power comes through electronic fuel injection, multiple coil packs, and even dual overhead cams. Stock cars are then fitted with (amongst other things) V-8 power, rear wheel drive, and a distributor that triggers an analog-based ignition control.

This is not to say that stock car racing doesn't embrace technology. In fact, it takes a serious amount of engineering and research for these teams to achieve the speeds and RPM that they are able to with the caps that the rules mandate. Materials and the components these teams have worked to develop with the aftermarket have certainly advanced the entire industry. But one area that has not been welcomed

in the pits is digitally controlled ignition controls.

NASCAR rules allow only analog ignition systems, and the trigger signal must come from the distributor. Even when Crane first got into ignition systems, and only offered digital units, they finally developed an analog control so they could get into the NASCAR garages!

MSD's premiere ignition for high-end circle track racing is the 6 HVC Professional Racing Ignition. The ignition was designed to provide higher output while surviving in the nasty environment of stock car racing. One thing both ignitions share are Weatherpak Connectors, which are mandated by NASCAR in their rulebook. Also, a clear epoxy must be used so tech inspectors can take a look inside the control if they deem it necessary. This unit does not have a rev limiter built in, but is fit with a special connecter that plugs

Crane had to forego their digital controls to fit NASCAR's rules, resulting in the HI-6N Ignition. The unit features a single-stage rev limiter and conforms to other rules and regulations of the sanctioning body. MSD offers a series of ignitions designed for circle trace racing as well.

directly into a matching external rev control that is available separately.

the street/strip cars keeps advancing as more of these features trickle down from the higher-output racing applications and controllers. Speaking of higher-output ignitions, that is where we're getting, right after we mention one other popular timing retard option.

BOOST RETARD

Another feature a lot of street/strip cars will find useful in an ignition control is a boost retard circuit. This obviously will be of use only on engines that are being force-fed air and fuel through a supercharger or turbocharger. As boost pressure increases, so do cylinder pressures. This can result in detonation, which can rob you of performance, or worse yet, end up damaging the engine.

The MSD 6BTM (Boost Timing Master) ignition delivers the same performance and features as their 6AL, including the rev limiter, but it also includes the addition of a boost sensing circuit. To use the boost retard, a line

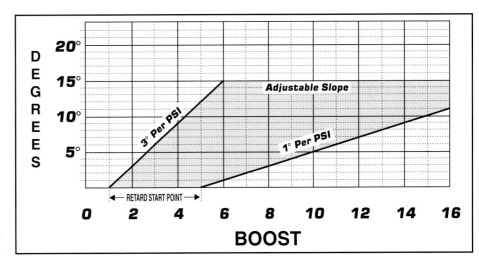

This chart illustrates the amount of timing retard that you can dial-in in relation to the boost pressure in the manifold. MSD's 6BTM lets you adjust from 0°-3° of retard per pound of boost. Also, you can adjust the amount of boost that must occur before the retard begins.

must be routed from the intake manifold to an inlet port on the side of the ignition so it can sense the pressure. There is also a control knob that you mount on the dash that lets you adjust the timing

retard from the driver's seat. This dial is marked of from 0° – 3°, and lets you adjust how many degrees of retard will occur per pound of boost. As an example, it your blower produces 7 psi, with

Most of Crane's HI-6 ignition controls are set up to provide a boost retard feature with the addition of a manifold absolute pressure (MAP) sensor and their TRC-2 Timing Control.

Manifold absolute pressure sensors are required to take advantage of a boost retard features of the Crane and Mallory ignitions. You'll need to run a boost line or quality fuel line from the intake manifold to the sensor. The three terminals are a signal output, voltage input, and ground.

the dial set on 2°, you would have a maximum of 14° of retard (7 x 2 = 14).

If you plan on one day adding a blower to your car, you may as well step up to one of these ignition controls from the get-go. You don't have to use the retard feature until you need it, so planning ahead can save you money in the long run. Most of the Crane Fireball HI-6 heries ignition controls have a retard circuit built-in them that can be used by adding a manifold absolute pressure (MAP) sensor and their TRC-2 Retard Control. This is a compact dial control that you install on the dashboard so you can make timing adjustments while driving! Mallory also has a similar upgrade feature built into their HyFire VI that you can take advantage of by adding a harness and a MAP sensor.

Multi Retard Function

Crane's TRC-2 Retard accessory retard dial control gives you several options other than just a boost retard. It will provide up to 20° of retard in its boost mode, plus it can also be used as an adjustable retard that is active constantly, or as a step retard that can be turned on only when desired.

On the compatible Fireball ignitions, a Yellow wire on the control box determines its use. When this wire is connected to ground, the retard is active at all times, giving you the opportunity to retard the timing whenever you feel it necessary — such as in times of heavy detonation. It can also be used as a step retard, which is common when a stage of nitrous is activated. This can be done by wiring a relay to supply a ground path on the yellow wire when the nitrous solenoid is activated.

For a retard that is proportional with boost pressure, the yellow wire does not need to be connected and should be sealed. The TRC-2 goes into boost retard mode once you connect it to Crane's MAP sensor (supplied with matching harness). Rather than a 20° span, the control knob now registers increments of 0 – 4° per pound of boost. The Crane unit accepts a maximum of 15 psi and will retard a maximum of 20°.

Once you wire the TRC-2 to your ignition, Crane recommends setting it to 0° and rechecking the timing.

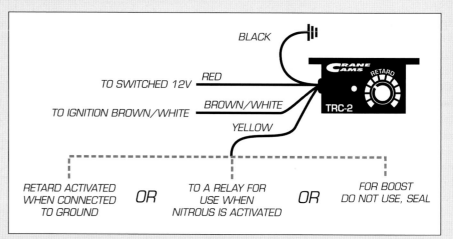

Crane's TRC-2 retard dial can be used for boost retard, a step retard, or a continuous retard, depending on how it is wired. When the yellow wire is connected to ground, the retard is activated. It can be used as a continuous retard, a step retard, or add a MAP sensor and seal the wire for a boost-proportional retard.

THE NEXT STEP — THE 7-SERIES

When you get a little more serious about performance and expect a little more impact from your ignition, you enter the 7-Series zone. Again, the 7 is more of a designation than having any specific connotation to the ignition's operation or the applications they are used on. It's just the way it has been for a long time and the manufacturers and racers seem to know what a 7-Series relates to. (If it ain't broke...)

The 7-Series ignitions from Crane, Mallory, and MSD are designed for engines with higher compression, big-lift cams, high-flowing heads and intakes, big carbs or injectors, and lots

The MSD 7AL-2 was a popular choice for drag racing engines for a long time. On paper, it doesn't appear to deliver any more spark energy than their 6AL, but its circuits produce a different spark profile with extremely quick recovery characteristics, which made it a great choice for engines with high compression and cylinder pressure. This racer was wired in a timing control with their 7AL-2.

Coil selection will have an impact on the spark that makes it to the combustion chamber. There are many different characteristics designed into a coil that will determine its efficiency and how it will work with different ignitions. We'll take a closer look at coils throughout Chapter 4.

The Fireball HI-7 is Crane's offering for drag racers looking for more spark energy. The ignition is supplied with the harness and a capacitor to help filter the supply voltage and protect against voltage spikes.

The HyFire VII-S from Mallory is designed with sportsman racing in mind. It delivers great spark energy and voltage, plus it has a built-in LED screen that lets you scroll through and set options such as two rev limiters, a single retard, and a starting retard to ease cranking.

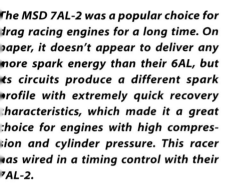

of nitrous or boost pressures. In short, 7-Series ignitions are meant for high-powered engines! Most of these ignitions produce higher spark energy and increased primary voltage to the coil. To deliver more power, these ignitions will also suck more current and voltage from the battery, so you have to make sure your charging system and/or battery are in great working order. Also, most of these ignitions are not legal for use on pollution-controlled vehicles, not that they're exactly intended for extended use on the street anyway!

Knowing exactly just when you need to step up to a 7-Series ignition system is not a clear-cut case. The 6-Series ignitions hold their own through so many applications, and the newest additions in recent years are even more powerful and efficient. If you already are running a 6-box of some sort and continue to modify your engine to make more power, deciding when to move to a 7 Series is a tough call. On naturally aspirated engines, compression can be used as an indicator. MSD recommends that on engines with over 12:1 compression, the 7-Series ignition begin to look like the route to go. In their Fireball ignition catalog, Crane lists their HI-6's to provide enough fire

to light up engines through 14.5:1 compression. It is noted that this is only the case when the ignition control is feeding their high-performance LX-92 coil. In recent years, coil technology has improved so coils can recover quicker, they're more efficient because of less loss during the high-voltage induction, and they run cooler. Many people have said that the MSD 7AL-2 couldn't be run on the street, but it was really their Pro Power Coil that limited the 7AL to the strip. We've seen these ignitions reliably power cars across the country when the correct coil is mated to the system. So be sure to pay attention to which coil the manufacturer recommends to match your application.

When you get to a point that your car is more of a strip/street car than street/strip car, it will be in your best interest to step up to these racing ignitions. Most of these ignitions are designed for drag strip use though we have seen 7AL's on circle track cars that run for under 50 laps. It is not common, and in some sanctions, they may not even be legal. (When you're talking about sprint cars, you get into magnetos, which we'll hit on in a few pages.)

To borrow from southern comedian Jeff Foxworthy, when you start to pipe in 200 additional horsepower from nitrous, you might just need a 7-Series ignition. If you have a blower that's

putting over 15 pounds of boost into the manifold, you may find yourself looking for a 7-Series ignition. If your pistons are domed so high that they look like upside down cereal bowls with valve recesses built in, you might be in need of a... well you get the idea. In short, the 7-Series ignitions are the most popular series when it comes to drag racing applications.

Mallory offers three versions of their HyFire VII-C series ignitions. All of them produce the same powerful CD sparks while it is their accessories offerings that set them apart. The only difference between the PN 667C and the

Instead of having the LED and push buttons on the ignition control, Mallory also offers the HyFire VII-C series, which uses a remote digital controller connected through a removable computer harness to make your adjustments. This way you don't have to have the ignition mounted so you can view the screen.

MSD offers a Digital-7 ignition that has built-in rotary dials to set its two rev limits and a step retard. They also offer a Programmable Control that is chock full of accessories and programmable features that can be set using a laptop computer.

The Programmable Digital-7 from MSD can be programmed with their optional hand-held monitor that allows you to scroll through an LCD screen to set its functions. If you plan on getting tricky with your programming, it is best to connect your laptop and use their Pro-Data+ software to whittle through your programming.

667CR is that the CR offers four steps of retards instead of two with the PN 667C. The third unit is the PN 667BTR, which offers the ability to retard the timing in relation to boost pressure through a 3-Bar MAP sensor that is supplied. This feature is ideal of blown and turbo applications, plus there is still the three step retards and three rev-limiting stages.

Did you notice that as the ignitions are used more for racing applications they also have more accessories built-in? This is also a common theme with digital controls. A few years ago, MSD stepped up their 7AL-2 by adding a few features such as three rev limits, four retards, and an RPM-activated switch. This ignition, deemed the 7AL-3 (didn't see that coming, did you?), also had improved power output over the standard AL-2 and it was, and still is, an analog ignition control.

Since then, the folks at MSD have developed their own Digital-7 line of controls. The base unit shares the same features and controls as their Digital-6+ ignition, except its circuits produce a much higher spark energy and primary voltage to the coil. This is accomplished by choosing different power-making components within the ignition. The base Digital-7 provides two rev limits, a step retard, and a starting retard. For engines that use electronic fuel management systems, this is a good choice because you won't pay for programmable features that you don't need, since so many adjustments can be made through the ECU.

If you find yourself in need of more accessories, you'll have to look to their Programmable Digital-7 Ignition controls. There are now a couple different versions of this ignition, but at this point, we'll be discussing their original version. This ignition control delivers the same output as their standard Digital-7+ unit but offers a cornucopia of tuning opportunities. We will get into more of these tuning and programming capabilities later in the book, but to give you an idea, you can set three rev limits, three retard steps, an RPM-activated switch, map out a complete timing curve for the run and during the holeshot, adjust the timing of each cylinder, and much more.

MSD developed a Windows-based software for their line of programmable ignitions and accessories (which is free from their website). If you're a serious racer, but a little leery about computers

PC Programmable

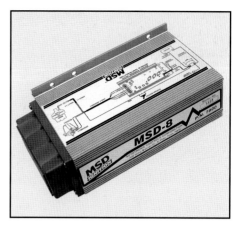

MSD's Programmable Digital-7 is used in a variety of classes ranging from Pro Stock to Radial Tire classes as racers take advantage of the programs that fit their needs. Last year, MSD released two more versions of the Programmable Digital-7, one with a boost retard feature, PN 7535, and the other is called the Plus model, PN 7531. Both were treated to a few the new features and programs that could be adjusted.

The Boost model of course offers racers the ability to set a retard curve in proportion to manifold pressure. There were also some other features added including timing curves for each gear. The Plus version was fit with an absolute plethora of programs including a few that were well received with racers, but not with a couple sanctioning bodies. The Plus has a new kind of rev limiter built into it, called a slew rate rev limiter. This limiter is actually based on a ratio of engine RPM and time so you program a rev limiter that controls the engine's rate of acceleration per second. This is feature along with several others left NHRA and IHRA tech crews in a bit of a quandary. To make a long story short, the Plus was deemed illegal for use in all NHRA and IHRA classes (whether or not that was changed for the 2004 season, consult their rule books).

The MSD 8 has always been a favorite of tractor and truck pullers. This analog-controlled ignition produces a great amount of current and voltage energy, but it also requires a steep amount of supply voltage from the battery.

Can there be such a thing as too much ignition tuning? Apparently so! The NHRA and IHRA felt there was and banned the use of MSD's Programmable Plus, PN 7531, from use. Their Programmable Digital-7, PN 7530, however, is legal in both racing organizations.

...nd programs, get over it. It's time to ...ealize that a laptop is an important tool ...n drag racing, whether you're down-...oading data from acquisition equip-...nent, or programming a cylinder-...o-cylinder timing curve, you better get ...vith the program. Since the time this ...ook went to print, there are probably ...new ignitions available (or will be soon) ...hat can be programmed through a lap-...op. Once you learn to take advantage of the advanced tuning that you can achieve, there will be no going back.

OVER-THE-TOP IGNITION POWER

What else do you consider a tractor puller with three blown-alcohol injected engines or a turbocharged small-block Ford that runs the quarter mile under six seconds at 200 mph plus? These applications are simply over-the-

top, and fortunately, there are ignition controls that climb right over the top as well, and they can deliver the spark energy that is needed.

Again, in thinking like a racer, a 7-Series ignition is pretty darn powerful, but an 8-Series must be even better! Thus, we introduce the MSD 8 ignition control. This analog controlled race-only ignition creates more and more energy to maintain a powerful spark across the plug gap in the most unforgiving environment. With the advent of move powerful magnetos, the MSD 8s have never been a popular ignition, but you see a few here and there, especially in pulling competitions. To make the kind of power they deliver, they suck up a lot of supply current and voltage, which makes it tough on race engines with limited battery resources.

MSD skipped right over any of thought of a 9-Series ignition when they developed the MSD 10-Plus. This ignition system is unique in that it is actually a CD ignition and an inductive ignition. In Chapter 2 we mentioned how the sparks of both ignition systems have their own benefits, and the MSD 10-Series lets you have your cake and eat it too.

When it was first introduced, the MSD 10 used two coils. One was a CD-style coil, the other was an inductive design that favored long-spark dura-

Magnetos

You'll find the MSD 10-Series ignitions on high-end Pro Street and Pro Outlaw engines. The 10 combines a CD spark and an inductive spark to produce the ultimate spark profile. It has great initial voltage to ionize the spark plug gap, followed with plenty of energy for long spark duration in the cylinder. Note the two coils.

tion. The two spark profiles were combined using MSD's patented technology to deliver a high-voltage spark of a CD ignition with the long, fuel-burning energy of an inductive spark. As their coil building technology advanced, they were able to design a single coil that could handle both sparks. The single coil system is known as the 10-Plus.

The MSD 10 and 10-Plus are used primarily on drag cars that are either gulping excessive amounts of nitrous, or have insane amounts of boost pressure from a blower or turbo. Many of these cars are producing over 35 pounds of boost, and these racers need an ignition up to the task. Obviously, these last few ignitions are not for everyone. One racer explained that it allowed them a little extra margin of error in their tune up, because these over-the-top ignitions could handle it. With the way these cars are using nitrous and with the advancements in forced induction systems, there comes a need to retard the timing back close to top dead center (TDC). Hence, there may be more excessive ignition systems in the near future.

There is yet another step when looking at ignition controls for engines that are on the ragged edge of performance. The magneto is another style of ignition that will fire the spark plugs, but they're a whole different ball of wax. And they aren't something you find on street cars or even drag cars, until you get into burning alcohol and nitro, or sprint cars.

One of a magneto's main advantages is that it makes its own power, so a big heavy 12-volt battery doesn't need to be mounted in the car. A magneto is actually an inductive ignition design. They are constantly generating current that is controlled through breaker points or electronic circuits to turn the current on and off. They can produce a lot of current with a long duration, plus are self-contained for the most part.

Magnetos have their advantages, but there are reasons you don't see them on street or mild strip cars. For starters, there is the cranking RPM. To make enough current for a quality spark, a magneto must spin at a high rate, and some block-mounted starters could have trouble with the locked out timing and engine heat. Also, magnetos never had the ability to incorporate timing controls, rev limiters, and other controls that racers crave (though the MSD Pro Mag system gives racers these opportu-

nities). Space can be another hurdle for the magneto, as most of the generators are tall and bulky. With all the improvement in battery technology, and with all the electronics that racers use these days, it's no wonder that most cars have some sort of a battery to power fuel or water pumps and acquisition controls.

MSD started offering their Pro Mag nearly 10 years ago. They offer a Pro Mag 12, which is a 12-amp version that is popular in sprint cars and other circle track classes. They also offer a hefty 44-amp Pro Mag that is used on Top Fuel and Funny Cars as well as some alcohol classes. The nitro classes use two complete 44-amp systems! How's that for power? MSD's magnetos use a magnetic pickup, which has allowed many teams to move to crank trigger systems and incorporate electronic timing controls. Top Fuel cars have embraced this technology and are manipulating the timing over 15 times within a 4.5-second pass!

We have seen a few race teams that are running an MSD Pro Mag on their turbocharged outlaw street cars. As boost pressures and this technology continue to grow, maybe we'll see more racers go this direction. Then again, as CD ignition technology continues to blossom, there may not be a need to switch to a magneto!

Mallory, Vertex, MSD, Don Zig, and Joe Hunt are just a few of the names you'll see on the sides of magnetos. Magnetos are used mostly in hard-core racing applications such as sprint cars, alcohol engines, and Top Fuel classes.

The MSD Pro Mag 44 is used to fire the volatile mixtures that Top Fuel racing demands. These generators deliver 44 amps to their special coils with an Electronic Points Box controlling the energy. Note the two complete magnetos!

COILS, WIRES, AND PLUGS
Take a Look at the Secondary Side

The previous chapters explained how you could improve your car's performance by adding a performance ignition control to the primary side of the ignition. Now we'll take a look at the secondary, or high-voltage side of things.

The result of an aftermarket ignition is an improved spark through enhanced dwell control, upping the lev-

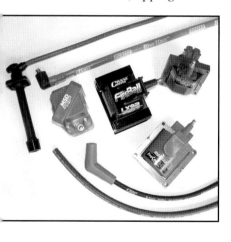

There are a lot of components available to improve the performance and operation of the secondary side of the ignition system. Coils that promise huge voltage numbers or longer spark duration will improve combustion. Also, wires with the lowest resistance will deliver more current to improve combustion. Which ones are right for your ignition and application?

el of the primary voltage, and sometimes both. All of these systems work great, but one thing that is certain, is that they cannot do it alone. These ignitions still rely on the coil to make them shine. The coil steps up the voltage that an ignition (or battery) supplies to an amount that will ignite whatever fuel is in the combustion chamber. It also has to accomplish these goals with great speed, efficiency, and repeatability. A lot more goes into building a coil than most people realize.

Not to take anything away from the rest of the secondary side of the ignition. The coil wire that delivers the voltage to the distributor cap performs eight times the duty of the other plug wires. All of the plug wires have to handle thousands of volts with plenty of spark energy. Not only do they have to get the spark to the plugs, they also need to suppress the electrical interference that comes with traveling voltages. Plus, look at the environment they have to work in! Sweltering heat, moving components, and even gale force winds whipping them around. They have to grip the spark plug through thick and thin to make sure the voltage makes it to the plug gap where it ionizes a path for the current to follow.

So you can see that there's a lot happening on the secondary side of the ignition system. We'll take a closer look

at these components, starting with the coil, where the high voltage is created.

COILS

The coil of the ignition system is where magic is used as 12 volts from the battery go into the primary terminals, and thousands of volts are released through secondary tower. Okay, we all know that magic isn't responsible for this phenomenon. It is all in the hands of electrical theory and laws of physics, even though many would still like to believe that a coil is like a magic hat. Once you see how the voltage is stepped up and the operation of the coil, you'll understand the different specifications and why certain coils can only be used for certain applications.

Inside a coil there are two sets of windings: a primary and a secondary set. The primary windings are connected to the battery and therefore can be considered the final step in the primary side of the ignition system. These primary windings are generally hundreds of windings and are connected between the positive and negative terminals of the coil. The secondary windings are made up of thousands of windings with a finer wire material. These windings are connected to the secondary tower of the coil and the coil primary terminal. Both sets of windings are positioned

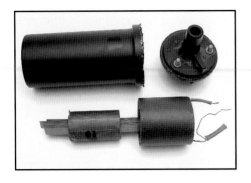

This shows the inside of a standard canister coil. The core material varies, but serves the same purpose to help build up the magnetic field. Also note that different shapes and architecture will affect a coil's performance.

around an iron (or similar metal) core that improves the strength of the magnetic field that occurs.

When current flows through the primary windings, a magnetic field is produced. When this flow is stopped by the trigger signal, such as when the points open, the voltage is induced into the secondary windings. Due to the increased number of windings that make up the secondary side, a step up in voltage is produced. This is where a few volts are turned into the thousands of volts that fire the plug.

If you've shopped around for a performance coil or have looked at coils on different cars at shows or races, you've no doubt noticed that there are a lot of different coils available! Even if you're looking through one ignition company's catalog, you'll see there are a variety of coils offered ranging from stock replacement housings to special, race-only coils. This wide range is because there can be a lot of things altered within a coil to give it different characteristics. These differences can be an advantage to certain ignition systems, or conversely, a problem to others. There are a lot of variables to a coil and making sure that you get the right one for your ignition and application is important to its final output.

Turns Ratio

The relationship between the primary and secondary windings is commonly referred to as a turns ratio. This is

a coil specification that you'll see in most catalogs or ads. Since the secondary windings consist of thousands of loops, you'll see them compared to the primary as 100 secondary turns to every one primary turn for a ratio of 100:1. When there are 12 volts going into the coil and the trigger breaks the flow of the current, there is typically a voltage spike. This spike in the primary windings may reach up to 250 volts or more before it is induced into the secondary windings. When there is a turns ratio of 100:1, the voltage is multiplied 100 times, creating a spark output of 25,000 volts.

This is of course the theory on paper. There are many obstacles that can affect the output number, such as the heat in the coil and loss that occurs during induction. But the equation works as a general rule of thumb when talking turns ratios and voltage outputs.

Engineers can alter the secondary output by modifying the turns ratio of the coil. For instance, if the same materials were used to make a coil with a 75:1 ratio, the output voltage would be down to 18,750 volts. Or, what if the ratio was increased to say 120:1, the secondary voltage would be 30,000 volts! All of this voltage sounds great and easy to accomplish, but there is a catch. As

Performance replacement coils that fit factory brackets and connectors are now available for many popular applications. These coils may share the same housing as the stock one, but they're designed with improved materials and may have different windings to produce more output.

Though these two Moroso coils look identical, there are substantial differences internally. One is designed for use with an inductive ignition, while the other is directed towards CD ignition systems. You can get away with an inductive coil with a CD ignition, but not vice-versa.

the voltage output is increased, the amount of current output is decreased. Likewise, as voltage is lowered, current increases. Of course, just how much these properties teeter-totter is dependent on the materials used and the make-up of the coil itself. It's a catch-22, and a middle ground must be found!

Ignition companies have to face this compromise head on, especially when it comes to offering coils for use on street cars with inductive ignitions, for mild use with CD ignitions, and for engines that see high RPM for long amounts of time. Many of the entry-level coils will deliver good performance in a middle-of-the-road designed coil. There are also coils that are designed more for the slower voltage build up and long duration of an inductive ignition, while others will be designed to handle the high-voltage wallop that a CD ignition delivers. There are many things that come into play.

Resistance

Resistance is what works against the current. It is measured in a unit called ohms. It can be used to increase the flow of the spark energy or decrease it. Coils can be wound with different materials and in manners to alter the resistance of the primary and secondary windings, thereby modifying the output of the coil. Generally thicker material produces less resistance, which also means less heat. Of course, thicker material means a larger coil!

The primary windings will have a much lower resistance value than the secondary windings. Generally, the primary resistance of any coil will be under 2 ohms; in fact, it's usually in the tenths or even hundredths of an ohm in the case of coils designed for high-end CD ignitions. By having lower resistance, more current will be in the windings when the field is collapsed and induced into the secondary windings.

Since there are thousands more windings on the secondary side of the coil, there's bound to be more resistance. Depending on the coil, there may be 100 ohms or anywhere up to 10,000 ohms! That's quite a variance, but again it depends on what the coil is designed to operate with. Not to mention, the windings must fall within the given specs of the turns ratio as well. There is no way to make one adjustment in a coil's build up without affecting several other specifications.

Inductance

Another common specification you'll see for coils is inductance. The transfer of voltage and energy from one set of windings to the other is called inductance. It is measured in a property called Henrys and in the case of most automotive coils, this will be in milli-Henrys (mH).

Inductance is related to the charge time or rise time of a coil. That is, the amount of time it takes for the voltage to be induced and stepped up through the secondary windings. The lower the inductance value, the faster the rise time. In high-end applications, changing from a high-inductance coil (slow rise time) to a low-inductance coil, the actual timing can be affected at higher RPM. If a coil doesn't take as long to induce a voltage, especially at higher RPM, you may see an advance in the timing. To see a timing change, there must be substantial difference in the coils, but with the number of different coils available, it can happen. An important thing though is that you may not see this change occur while revving the car in the pits. There needs to be a load

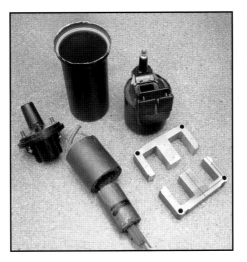

The internals of a canister coil are on the left while an E-core coil is on the right. E-core coils are more efficient in stepping up the voltage through the windings. Less loss, less heat, and a durable housing mean more power for you!

on the engine so the coil actually has to build up a higher amount of voltage. When the engine is just revving free, it doesn't take a lot of voltage to jump the plug gap, so the timing may not be affected as much.

Housing Design

In the past decade, there's been a lot more coil designs appear both from OEMs and from the aftermarket. You'll see in most performance applications that the coils have taken to more of a square look, or that they have at least have departed from the standard cylindrical or canister housing. This is due to advances in the way the primary and secondary windings are laid out in relation to the iron core.

The core in many of these coils resembles an "E" compared to just a straight piece of metal. This of course is why the coils are referred to as "E-core" coils. This design has proven to be more efficient in stepping up the voltage between the windings, due to a smaller and more enclosed area where the field collapses. Reducing the amount of leakage inductance, or the loss of energy, improves the coil's ability to transfer voltage and current to the secondary windings.

Another important aspect of a given

coil that must be considered is how well it cools. Canister coils are generally filled with oil to keep the windings cool during operation. E-core coils are more efficient, so there is generally less heat to dissipate, but they also produce more energy and voltage to begin with. Most of these coils use special heat-sinking materials to pull the heat out of the coil and into their grounded coil brackets and external housings. Another benefit to these epoxy-filled E-coils is the added vibration protection that is achieved by encasing all of the wiring, so they cannot succumb to excessive vibrations.

WHAT'S AVAILABLE?

As with ignition controls, there are a variety of coils offered from the aftermarket. All of them have several improved output replacement coils for the likes of the popular Ford TFI ignition, the dual connector GM coils, HEI coils, and even a few distributorless coil packs. The venerable canister coil is still offered in a variety of outputs and housings, but there are many other offerings these days. When it comes to performance, each company has its own way of thinking, its process for building a coil, as well as their own goals for what they want the coil to accomplish. With more of an understanding of how a coil works and what it can do, you can find the right one to

MSD and Moroso recommend routing a ground wire from the coil's bracket to ground on their HVC and Plasma Plus coils respectively. This extra ground is required to help suppress electro magnetic interference (EMI) and reduce the chance of shocks.

Ballast Resistor

When a breaker points distributor is used to open the primary coil circuit, there will be a ballast resistor or resistance wiring in line to the coil positive wire. This is necessary to lower the amount of voltage and current, which improves the longevity of the points. Most electronic triggers do not require the extra resistance because they can accept the increased current and voltage.

In the case that there is a ballast resistor in line to the coil's primary terminal, there may be a bypass wiring circuit that occurs during cranking. If there is a wire running from the starter solenoid to the coil's positive terminal, this is the case. This circuit is responsible for applying full battery voltage to the coil when the engine is cranking.

The intent is to create a hotter spark to improve starting. Once the engine fires and the key is moved back to the run position, the only voltage going to the coil is through the ballast where it is again regulated to a lower voltage, generally around 9.5 –10.5 volts.

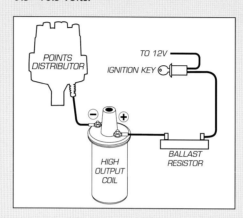

When some aftermarket coils are used with a points distributor there will need an extra ballast resistor. This is due to the coil's lower primary resistance, improved materials, and increased turns ratio. If one of these coils was used without the ballast, the points will wear and burn prematurely.

If you still are using a distributor with breaker points, an extra ballast resistor may be required to install a performance coil. The resistor will lower the voltage and current so the points won't be damaged.

The latest coil line from Crane is the LX line. These coils are smaller than their sibling PS versions. Their LX92 and PS92 models are designed exclusively for CD ignition systems while the 91 versions can be used on inductive systems.

MSD's HVC coil line consists of three different coils: a 6-series, 7-series, and one for their special 6-HVC Ignition. Add to that a second generation of HVC coils, the HVC II, and you have a lot of coils to choose from!

The Mallory 28880 Promaster model coil is designed for their CD systems such as the HyFire VII and X electronic ignition controls. It is ideal for high-RPM applications that run for a long time.

match your application.

In recent years, MSD has also added to their coil offerings. They are now building several of their coils in house, giving them more opportunities to evaluate different materials and winding procedures along the way. One of the coil series is called the HVC II. This is a second generation of sorts for

this line of coils. It stands for "high voltage and current," because the goal of these coils is to produce both high volts and amps instead of dealing with the trade off of one or the other. These coils have a serious amount of girth for a coil, but that is part of the reason that they produce such good numbers. Like a racer with a good cam, MSD doesn't

give out much info on the internals of any of their coils.

Mallory has also been evaluating and testing new coils in their labs. They still offer several canister coils

Troubleshooting Coils

There are not a lot of checks you can do to the ignition coil, especially in times of an intermittent misfire. A coil is one of those things that generally works or doesn't work without a lot of middle ground in between. Stranger things have of course occurred and being able to check a couple physical aspects of the coil will always help put your mind at ease.

You can check the primary and secondary resistance values of the coil, plus check to make sure they are not shorted to the housing or ground. Since there are so many different coil specifications, you'll need to consult with your coil's manufacturer to make sure everything is within spec. To check the primary resistance, simply connect an ohmmeter across the coil's negative and positive terminals. The reading will generally be under 1 ohm. The secondary resistance can be checked by connecting your meter to the coil's secondary tower and one of the primary terminals. Depending on your coil, this can measure any where from 30 to over 1,000 ohms! Also, check for continuity from the primary

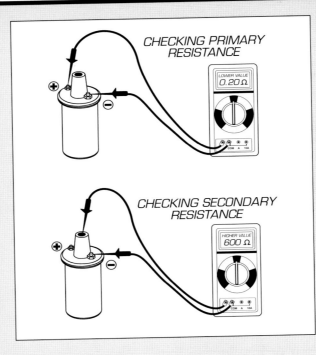

CHECKING PRIMARY RESISTANCE

LOWER VALUE 0.20 Ω

CHECKING SECONDARY RESISTANCE

HIGHER VALUE 600 Ω

You can check the primary resistance value of your coil by connecting an ohmmeter across the primary terminal. To check the secondary resistance, go from the secondary tower to primary positive terminals. Of course, you'll need to know your coil's specific specifications, since they vary from manufacturer to manufacturer.

and secondary terminals to the coil's housing or ground to make sure there are no shorts.

Also take a visual look around the secondary tower for signs of carbon tracking, which would be caused by sparks arcing. While you have your ohmmeter out, check the resistance of the coil-wire lead

to the distributor as well. Remember, this wire has to do eight times (or four or six) the work that the other wires do! If it has excessive resistance or an open, the voltage is going to find somewhere to get to ground, and that could mean jumping to the primary terminals or across to the engine.

---

and have increased their Promaster coil line with models for their Unilite distributors, for inductive systems, and even for high-RPM CD racing models. They also offer several E-core coils as Promaster E-Series for those same ignition designs.

The important thing to consider when selecting a coil is its compatibility with the ignition you are running. It is recommended to stick with one company for an ignition and a coil, since they were intended to operate together. This is more common in street cars because once you get into competitive racing situations, these teams will try anything to get an inch ahead. If they find a different coil gives them two more horse-power with a different ignition control,

you can bet they're going to run with it. Always contact the manufacturer if you have coil compatibility concerns.

SPARK PLUG WIRES

You can have the best coil and ignition controls available, but they won't do you any good if the spark plug wires aren't up to the task of handling all their energy and voltage. Good plug wires are needed in all ignition systems, even distributorless ignition systems. As usual, there are exceptions as there are now coil-on-plug systems on some factory applications. These systems have individual coils that are mounted just above the spark plug making the job of the plug wire obsolete. Again though,

for this discussion, spark plug wires are a very important part assembling a performance ignition system.

When voltage travels through the spark plug wire, a field is created. This magnetic field can wreak havoc on other electronics in your car, such as rev limiters, timing controls, and even the ECU. To combat this electro magnetic interference (EMI), or noise, a spark plug wire must use a conductor that has the ability to suppress this noise. This is why spark plug wires have resistance.

OEM's have been using spark plug wires with a carbon core for quite a few years. This carbon core serves as an adequate conductor, but it offers very high noise suppression capabilities. The trouble is that carbon core wires generally

Modified Caps for Better Coils

On many Honda and Acura engines, the coil is inside the distributor cap. To fit inside, the coil is tiny, plus it contends with engine heat while being locked under the cap. These coils work fine for thousands of miles on thousands of cars that get driven every day. Again though, this isn't a repair manual, it's a performance book! When you're looking to upgrade a Honda's ignition output, a coil upgrade is a perfect place to start.

Since the coil is inside the distributor, these systems do not have a coil wire or secondary tower on the cap. How are you supposed to get the voltage from the new externally mounted coil to the rotor? With a modified cap of course!

Crane and MSD offer several caps for different Honda applications that

These Honda distributor caps from Crane are fit with a secondary coil tower. The terminal is connected to a brass terminal that runs to the rotor tip. A cap like this is necessary when you move from the factory in-cap coil to an external coil with improved output.

If you can't find a modified cap for your application, you may be able to modify your own cap. MSD offers the Power Tip that you can install in your own cap.

are fit with a secondary coil tower. This provides a path for the high voltage of the

coil to be transferred to the rotor tip and on to the spark plugs.

HEI Hop Up

The GM HEI distributor uses a coil that is mounted inside its cap. This is an efficient design for stock vehicles and a favorite to many street rodders due to its simplicity. However, having the coil inside the cap can limit the voltage output potential due to size constraints and heat.

There are of course, a variety of aftermarket coils available that will bolt right in the cap. Some coils are designed to work with a stock or mild upgrade in the ignition module, such as the models available from Crane and Moroso. Some other coils may be matched to a company's specific performance HEI module. When you're swapping from a factory coil to an aftermarket, make sure to use a coil that has the same color wires that lead to the cap connector.

MSD's HEI Coil is designed to fit in place of the stock coil and even looks exactly the same. Looks can be deceiving though, and MSD only recommends using their HEI coil with their high-output HEI ignition module.

Some companies offer kits that allow you to remove the factory HEI coil and adapt an external coil to provide the high voltage. This is done by having an extension that leads from the center terminal rotor button out to a secondary tower.

There is another choice, besides just replacing the HEI with another HEI-style coil, and that is to remove it completely! Several companies offer a modified cover

for the HEI that is made to transfer the high voltage from the coil to the rotor. This way you can run a coil with higher output that can be mounted outside.

Radio Noise Info

The only noise you ever want to hear coming out of your car's stereo speakers better be that one lame song stuck between your two favorites. If you're getting an annoying buzz through the speakers with the radio on, it could be noise coming from the secondary side of the ignition (specifically, the plug wires).

Radio Frequency Interference (RFI) will be noticeable largely on the AM band and slightly through FM stations. This is one reason you need a good quality spark plug wire! If you just installed a set of wires, then notice a noise through your favorite tune, you should check out the installation. Another thing you can do is to get

A noise filter for the ignition and some dielectric grease can help diminish radio frequency interference.

some dielectric grease from one of the ignition companies and apply a dab or

two on the plug boots and terminals. This helps reduce voltage leaks. Also make sure there's a good ground from the engine to the chassis, and the stereo to the chassis as well.

If the noise is also audible when you're playing a tape (does anyone have tapes any more?) or a CD, then the culprit is more likely supply-line interference. For supply line interference, installing a noise filter or capacitor (again available from all the manufacturers) on your new ignition's power leads will help. Not only can this help reduce noise, it also protects the ignition from voltage spikes and current surges.

Solid core wires will deliver the most voltage and energy possible, but they cannot suppress electro magnetic interference (EMI) at all. On race engines without electronics or on an older engine like this inline-six Chevy, EMI isn't going to cause too many problems.

have extremely high resistance. We're talking thousands of ohms per foot! High resistance means that the flow of the ignition's current is not optimum and could be cutting into the amount of voltage that reaches the spark plugs.

Before there were so many electrically controlled components on race

cars, having a solid core wire was the ticket. Solid core wires have no resistance, so you knew that the most energy possible was reaching the spark plug gap. Trouble started to arise with the addition of higher-output ignitions, electric water and fuel pumps, electric fans, data acquisition, rev limiters, timing controls, and other electronic devices. All of a sudden, the carrying capabilities of solid core wires were fraught with noise interference.

Spiral Wound Wires

The answer is of course to use a spark plug wire that incorporates materials with resistance and that are designed to help suppress EMI. This sounds easy enough, but the trouble is that when a wire's resistance goes up, it reduces the amount of voltage and current that makes it to the spark plug. As resistance in the wire goes down, you increase the chances of EMI occurring. It's another one of those back and forth ignition system quandaries! The answer is a wire designed with lower resistance that can still suppress EMI; a wire that lets you have the best of both worlds. Is that too much to ask for? Not any more! Companies have found ways to

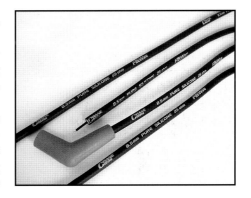

Crane's FireWire has only 25 ohms of resistance per foot, but still has high suppression capabilities. Crane's wire features a silicone jacket to handle high heat. They also offer it with a special heat sleeve for even more protection.

deliver a wire with lower resistance and higher suppression capabilities. These wires are referred to as helical- or spiral-wound plug wires.

The conductor material, generally a stainless steel, nickel, or copper alloy, is actually wrapped around a center core. This center section of the core is made up of different materials designed to improve suppression capabilities. Most of the premium performance wires available will promote a core that is fer-

Building a Wire

You can buy a set of custom-made wires for your application, but when you want a set that is routed exactly how you want it to be, you'll need to go with a universal set and build 'em yourself.

Most of the universal sets offered are supplied with the spark plug side terminal and boot installed. This is good as you'll get the benefits of a strong factory crimp on the end you pull off and on often. The terminals and boots for the distributor side are supplied loose so you can cut each wire to your exact length.

Cutting, stripping, and crimping the wires correctly is imperative to the performance and life of your new wires. Most universal sets are supplied with a crimping tool of sorts that is designed to live through one or maybe two sets of wires. These will do, but if you plan on ever making more wires, you'll need to invest in a good quality crimping tool. Moroso and MSD offer great tools that also have replaceable jaws, so you can use the tool for other wiring purposes also. A few wire building tips:

- Use extreme care not to damage or cut into the conductor. Any break in the conductor could promote an area for voltage to leak.
- When stripping the sleeve, after cutting it, rotate the cut portion

Most universal kits are supplied with a crimp tool that requires a vise or set of pliers. Investing in a quality crimp tool like this one from Moroso will make your custom wires better and save you time and effort.

DUAL CRIMP TERMINAL

POSITION WIRE — 1/8"

PLUG WIRE

CRIMP FIRST

PLUG WIRE

CRIMP SECOND

PLUG WIRE

These diagrams show how to position the conductor when using a dual-crimp terminal.

clockwise as you pull it off. The sleeve is lightly joined to the conductor, and this will help remove it without damaging the conductor.

- Use a dab of dielectric grease, such as MSD's Spark Guard, to protect against moisture and voltage leaks, plus it will make assembly of the boot on the wire much easier.

- Do not over-crimp the terminal. You do not want the crimp tabs to tear into the sleeve. This will also promote an area for voltage to escape.
- After assembling a wire, check its resistance. Better to find a bad crimp now than once the wires are installed on the car.

rite impregnated or features a semi-reactive core element. This essentially means that the core has some degree of magnetic permeability, or to establish magnetic induction. Through winding the conductor around these special cores, an effective EMI choke or suppression capability is produced. This gives us lower resistance wires that will deliver higher spark energy, while retaining higher EMI suppression capabilities. These new wires are a win-win situation.

You'll find that there are a lot of wires available from the aftermarket,

and most of them do a pretty good job. You're not going to feel a difference in performance going from a 100-ohm/foot wire to a 25-ohm/foot wire. Most wires that are available range from under 1000 ohms/foot to Crane's low 25-ohm/foot FireWire. This is the most important part of a wire, not the advertised thickness of the sleeve.

This is not to say that the sleeve isn't important. Obviously, a thick outer sleeve is going to provide more protection to the conductor of the wire, but it is not going to affect the voltage-carrying properties. The outer sleeve of

the wire is indeed important in that it takes the brunt of the engine heat, abrasion, and your oily, dirty hands. Most wire manufacturers use a form of silicone or their own proprietary compound to make up the outer sleeve their wire. Under this sleeve there is another thick layer that adds greater electrical insulation to isolate the voltage. Here is one area that the thicker wires can offer increased dielectric strength. A variety of materials are used here, but the latest and greatest seems to be ethylene propylene diene monomer, or EPDM. That's more of an engineering term

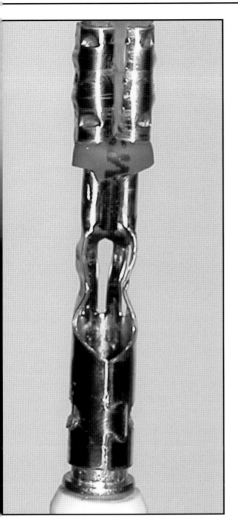

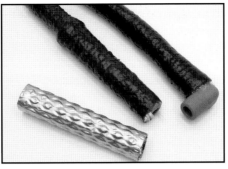

Burned boots are a problem in many engines, but there are steps you can take to slow the trouble. MSD offers a thick, silicone-covered, woven-glass sleeve that slides over the plug boots for more protection. They also offer Boot Armor, which is a shield made from stainless material that surrounds the boot.

These billet aluminum wire looms are great for street rods, but you're probably not going to see them on too many race cars.

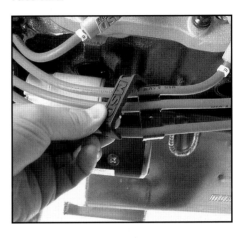

MSD uses special dual-crimp terminals to deliver a stout grasp on the wire. There are two sets of crimp tabs, one to grip the sleeve of the wire and the other to secure the conductor. These terminals also feature a locking tab that clicks onto the spark plug so you know when it is fully connected.

Moroso offers complete race prepped wire sets that already come with a heat sleeve installed. They even have cylinder number indicators.

These separators from MSD do a good job of securing the wires. They can be screwed in place and they hold the wires even when their locking top is removed, which makes replacing or removing a wire easy.

than something we understand completely, but the point is to look for a good quality wire from the inside out.

Having a roll of wire sitting on your workbench is not going to get the job of transferring voltage done. The wires need to have terminals and boots attached to each end, and that gives us another area to pay attention to while looking for wires. You want to make sure that the terminals will securely grip and lock to the spark plug and cap terminal. Nothing is worse that having a wire come off during a race. Well, yanking a terminal off the wire while trying

to remove it from the plug is almost as bad. Always twist the boot back and forth while pulling it off the spark plug!

Spark plug boots probably have one of the worst jobs of the ignition system. Boots need to handle extreme heat from headers and manifolds, plus keep the spark isolated so it goes into the spark plug rather than jumping to ground. All of the manufacturer's deliver good quality boots but some applications can just be brutal. MSD offers a boot designed to handle more heat. These Professional Race Boots as their called are made of a special material with a high de-vulcanizing rate that absorbs less radiation. This is just the tip of the iceberg in accessories for spark plug wires.

Accessories

Taking care of your wires by securing them from engine heat sources, adding extra heat sleeving, and even numbering your wires will help keep them, and your ignition's performance, in top condition. Most companies offer a variety of components to help you get the most out of your spark plug wires ranging from added boot protection to thick heat sleeves.

Moroso offers boot sleeves that are ideal for racing or even for use in a tow rig application. These sleeves are made from 3M Nextel, a woven ceramic material that can withstand extreme conditions without damage or becoming brittle. Mallory and Accel both provide rolls of a durable silicone and glass

A close visual inspection of your wires will give you clues to how they're holding up. Tears, cuts, or melted areas should be obvious, but also look signs of burned spots where a spark could jump to ground. You can also check the resistance of the wires. Check with the manufacturer to find out their resistance per foot value, but all of the wires should read close to each other.

woven sleeve that you slide over the wire for added heat and abrasion protection.

Another important part for your spark plug wires are separators. Routing and securing the wires from moving parts, hot engine components, linkage, and even other wires are very important to their performance and life. When you're at racing speeds, such as on a circle track car, there's a lot of wind under the hood that pushes and swirls around. Having the wires secure is an important step in bulletproofing the car. There are hundreds of separators available ranging from simple clips that hold the wires together to elaborate billet models that bolt down to the engine.

Wire Maintenance

Plug wires have their work cut out for them. They have to carry a high amount of voltage over a hot, volatile area. When there are no problems, the wires are forgotten and may go without being inspected or replaced over time. Depending on your application and what ignition system you are using, the plug wires should be considered a rou-

tine maintenance item. This is especially true of the coil wire as it works up to eight times more than the other wires.

On engines running an ignition such as a Crane HI-8 or an MSD Pro Mag, the plug wires carry a considerable amount of voltage and energy. Just like any other part on a race car, the wires will wear. Resistance could go up, cracks or breaks in the conductor could occur, and the terminals will wear from being pulled off and on during pit thrashes. How often you change your wires depends on how often the car is raced, but in extreme conditions, you'll want to inspect the wires every couple of events. For bracket cars and sportsman racing, maybe replace the entire wire set once throughout the year.

SPARK PLUGS

The last part of the secondary side of the ignition, and actually the end of the ignition cycle, is the spark plug itself. In the last few years the number of spark plugs available has grown in leaps and bounds. In performance applications for the most part, it seems that the most companies recommend a

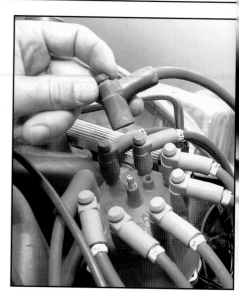

The plug wires need to be considered a maintenance item on your race car! If anything, at least replace the coil wire now and then. Which ignition system you use and how often you race will dictate when the wires should be replaced.

good quality standard-type spark plug. For daily driving, the multiple electrode versions and long lasting platinum designs can have their benefits. The best thing you can do is talk to your engine

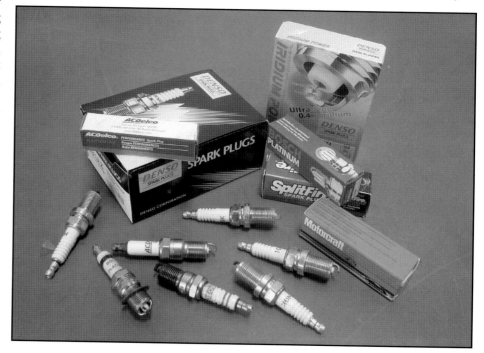

There are a lot of spark plugs available ranging from extended tips, multiple electrode models, cold or hot models, resistor plugs, and more. Which ones are ideal for your engine?

builder, fellow racers, and sniff around the websites or catalogs of the spark plug companies like Autolite, Denso, AC, Champion, Bosch, NGK.

The spark plug wire connects to the center terminal of the plug. The energy is transferred from the wire to its tip in the combustion chamber. From here, it jumps the gap to the electrode, which is grounded to the metal shell of the plug and to the cylinder head. Combustion of the air/fuel mixture occurs when the spark jumps the gap. In most passenger car spark plugs, there is a resistor in the center electrode that helps suppress EMI from interfering with the radio or other electronics on the vehicle. Race engines generally use non-resistor plugs, as they're not concerned with a little radio static. This is another reason why a good set of spark plug wires that help suppress noise are required. The shell of the housing is steel and provides a ground path between the electrode and the cylinder head. Heat is also transferred from the spark plug to the cylinder head through the shell.

Heat Range

You've probably heard about hotter and colder plugs, but an interesting note is that they really will not make a difference in your engine's performance output. But they can be of help when tuning, which means that using a hotter or colder plug may result in better numbers, so they are indirectly related to output. The best way for a plug to make a difference in power is by moving its position in relation to the piston.

The heat range of a plug refers to its ability to handle the thermal load that occurs from compression. You need a plug with a heat range that will rid itself of carbon deposits but won't create pre-ignition of the air/fuel mixture. If you use a plug that is too cold, you could be working towards early plug fouling due to excessive carbon build up.

Manufacturers determine the heat range of their plugs through different materials as well as through the design of the insulator. A hot plug will expose more of the insulator material so it absorbs and retains heat rather than transfer it to the cylinder head. A cold-

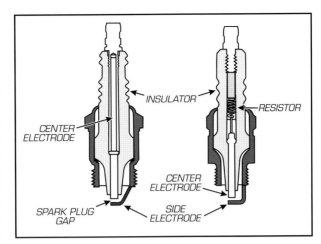

The cutaway of this plug illustrates that there's much more in the makeup of a spark plug than meets the eye. The center electrode must be well insulated and sealed to keep the spark from jumping to ground before it reaches the combustion chamber. Note the resistor in the center electrode on the plug to help reduce EMI.

er plug has less insulator material exposed to the combustion event, so more heat is transferred to the head. Generally, the higher the number on the spark plug, the hotter the plug. An R45TS AC plug is two-steps above an R43TS. Always start with a cooler plug if you're unsure, because if you're wrong in your choice, the plug will show signs of being rich which is a much better alternative than going too hot and experiencing detonation.

Typically, when you install a high-output ignition, you can step down to a colder spark plug, but it is not necessary. One change you can make in the plugs is their gap. Since your ignition now has the capability of producing higher voltage and current, opening the plug gap will expose more spark energy to the air/fuel mixture resulting in improved combustion and more power.

Plug Gap

Plug gap is an important setting. You want the gap as large as possible to get the most spark energy exposed between the electrodes. There is a point though that the gap can be too large and the spark has trouble jumping to the ground. This can be caused by a weak spark or by too much cylinder pressure. A plug gap of .045 inch is not going work well in a turbocharged engine that pounds 25 psi of boost into the cylinder. Cutting this gap down will be necessary, but the determining factor is the ability of the ignition.

As with timing specifications, it is difficult to for an ignition manufacturer

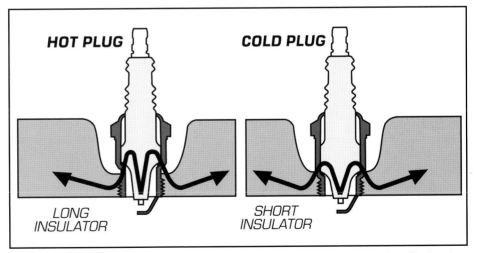

A colder spark plug will have a shorter insulator tip to promote quicker dissipation of the heat through the shell and ground of the plug. The longer insulator on a hotter plug is there to retain the heat. This makes the hotter plug more capable of keeping clean in a rich running engine.

Inspecting your plugs closely after a pass can give you an idea of what's going on in each cylinder. You can inspect each plug to help determine if its running lean or rich, and for signs of detonation. Driving the car back to the pits after a pass will spoil your attempts at reading the plugs.

Inspecting the insulator of the spark plug will tell you more about what is occurring in the cylinder. A magnifying tool like this one from Moroso will help you gain even more insight to the spark plug and inside the cylinder.

Indexing Plugs

Indexing the spark plugs determines the position of the electrode so it is in the best position to ignite the incoming fuel charge. On high-performance engines, it can also be necessary to provide clearance between a custom piston and the electrode. Many racers swear by indexing, yet others do not give it a second thought. Try it on your engine; you may like it!

If piston clearance is not the issue, then you want to position the electrode so it does not shield the spark from the incoming fuel mix. This can be accomplished with plug indexing washers such as from Moroso. These washers have different thickness, so the location of the electrode will be changed when the plug is torqued into the cylinder head. On the outside of the spark plug, mark the location of the electrode and install the spark plug to see where it ends up positioned. Then use the different washers to get your desired position.

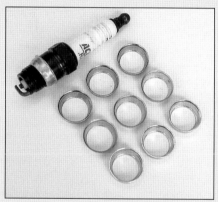

These indexing washers from Moroso will change the location of the electrode when you install the plug. A .010-inch washer will rotate the plug clockwise 105°, the .021-inch washer will achieve 210° of rotation, and the .032-inch washer will deliver 315° of rotation.

This indexing tool from Jones Racing Products will help you index a number of plug sets for your specific application.

to recommend a plug gap for every application. A typical street driven small-block Chevy can range from .030 -.050 inch. On blown alcohol applications, plug gaps may be as small as .015 inch. On your street/strip car, after installing a CD ignition control most of the manufacturer's recommend opening the plug gap a little bit. Start by opening it by .005 inch and test, and then try another .005 inch. When there is no longer a change in performance, go back .005 inch and call it good. If you see no improvement, stick with just a little wider than the original gap. Remember,

opening the gap will also put more pressure on the plug wires, cap, rotor, and coil wire.

Tuning With Spark Plugs

With the number of different spark plugs available and the variety of materials used in their production, it is difficult to explain exactly what to look for on your plugs. Also, the type of fuel you are using and even power adders like nitrous will affect the plug's appearance. There are obvious signs of fouling with carbon buildup or wet plugs, while

lean conditions will show extremely white with signs of detonation in excessive cases. Reading plugs is almost an art form, but it is also a valuable tool that you can learn with time and experience on your car.

Inspecting your plugs closely after a pass can give you an idea of what's going on in each cylinder. You can inspect each plug to help determine if it's running lean or rich, for signs of detonation. Driving the car back to the pits after a pass will spoil your attempts at reading the plugs.

DISTRIBUTOR BASICS
Triggers, Timing Advance, and Delivery

In most factory-type ignitions, the ignition cycle begins and ends with the distributor. One might say that the ignition goes full circle around the distributor, literally too.

The majority of cars being modified and updated for performance and racing still use a distributor to trigger the ignition system. There are of course, alternatives, such as crank triggered ignitions, which show up more on higher-performance race applications (though they still require a distributor to deliver the sparks). The use of distributorless electronic ignitions continues to grow, thanks in part to OEMs and several aftermarket manufacturers that offer high-performance components for a growing number of applications. These different systems will be covered in later chapters of this work. For now, we are going to concentrate on the workings of the run of the mill automotive distributor and its functions.

These common automotive distributors will have the following responsibilities:
- It will incorporate some sort of trigger device.
- Have the ability to alter the timing throughout changes in RPM and engine conditions.
- It will distribute the spark to the correct plug terminal at the right moment.

- Most distributors are responsible for driving the oil pump in the engine too.

Sounds simple enough right?

DISTRIBUTING

As its name implies, the distributor is responsible for distributing the spark

The distributor carries a lot of responsibility! It has to trigger the ignition at the exact moment, meet the changing needs of the engine, and then it has to deliver the spark to the right spark plug. Over the years, different trigger methods have been developed. There have been advances in trigger systems, the mechanical advance, and materials, but the overall methodology of a distributor has remained much the same.

from the ignition coil to the appropriate cylinder via its cap and the plug wires. To do this, the distributor shaft is driven by the camshaft through helically cut gears with a 1:1 ratio, so the distributor matches the one revolution of the camshaft. At the top of the distributor shaft is the rotor. On the majority of engines, the oil pump is also driven off the distributor shaft. This is accomplished through an intermediate shaft that connects to the distributor shaft at or below these gears.

When the coil releases the high secondary voltage, it is sent through the high-tension coil wire to the center terminal of the distributor cap. The end of this terminal has a carbon ball inside the distributor cap that is in contact with the center of the rotor's spring contact. This leads to a copper or brass tip that extends from the center to the rotor's outer edge. As the rotor spins, the voltage transfers over a small gap to the distributor cap terminal when they align. From here, the voltage shoots through the spark plug wire and to the spark plug, where it ionizes across the gap and ignites the air/fuel mixture. It sounds easy enough, but there is plenty that can go awry.

OEM distributors were made from an aluminum casting (or steel and iron way back when) and then fit with a bushing to support the shaft. Over time,

The majority of OEM distributors had bushings to guide the shaft. Most of the new billet aluminum distributors available from the aftermarket feature a ball bearing guide in the top housing. Some models have a bearing at the bottom also, or they use an extra-long sintered bushing.

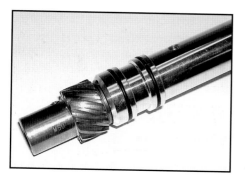

Some aftermarket billet-aluminum distributors can provide improved oil flow to the distributor gear. Optional O-rings on Chevrolet models will help control the oil flow by sealing off the lifter gallery. These O-rings can only be used when the block has been modified by chamfering the upper and lower edges of the distributor hole in the block.

this bushing will wear and possibly cause the shaft to wobble in the housing. Any wobble or worn areas can and will affect the timing. Top-of-the-line performance aftermarket distributors are generally CNC machined from bil-

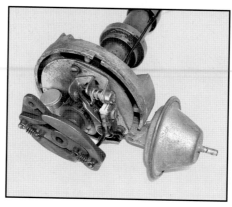

Millions of breaker point distributors have been produced and are still switching away on many cars. This worn distributor belongs in a 283-ci Chevrolet. The points are simply an on/off controller for the coil.

let aluminum to form a very strong and porous-free housing. Inside, there is usually a roller or ball bearing to support the distributor shaft. This design ensures smooth and accurate control of the distributor shaft.

If you cannot find a performance aftermarket distributor for your rare engine, or if you are a numbers-matching muscle-car fanatic and insist on using the stock distributor, make sure it spins true and that there is no excessive wobble or end play. There are still places where you can get new bushings or a new shaft installed to tighten up that original distributor. Look for them in Hemmings Motor News or other special vehicle publications or websites.

TRIGGERING THE IGNITION

The distributor, at least the models we're concentrating on for this discussion, must also trigger the ignition or coil. There are several different ways to accomplish this, like through mechanical breaker points or electronic switching devices, such as a magnetic pickup or Hall-effect switch. There are also optical triggers available. Whichever triggering path is followed, the goal is the same — to trigger the high voltage from the coil and to get it to the spark plugs at the exact moment in the compression stroke of each cylinder.

Breaker Points

Here we are in the 21st century and we're still discussing breaker points. Point systems are still being used in a lot of cars, and you can still get a brand new aftermarket distributor with points in it! The numbers of these distributors really isn't that out of order when you consider how many vehicles were produced with points providing the trigger. After all, it was the early 1970s before points were phased out by electronic triggers and systems. These days, finding a new set of points at the local auto parts store is getting tougher, and so is finding a counterman who understands what you're looking for! But points are still used and actually get the job done fairly well to a certain, shall we say, point.

Like the distributor itself, breaker points received their name directly from their vocation: breaking a circuit. The circuit they break is the primary current going into the coil by opening its ground path. The path that is broken is the lead that goes from the coil negative terminal to the points. When the points are closed, current is being delivered to the coil primary windings, creating a magnetic field. When the points open, or break the ground circuit, this field collapses to the secondary windings and a spark is sent out of the coil to the spark plugs.

On the distributor shaft, there is a cam with eight flat areas and eight lobes. The switching arm of the points is spring-loaded and has a rubbing block attached that rides against the cam. Each time a lobe comes up, it pushes the rubbing block, which opens the points contact and creates the trigger signal. Notice that when this happens, the rotor tip is also aligned with a terminal of the distributor cap to transfer the voltage to the spark plug wire.

Breaker points were used for decades and you really can't deny their ability to get the job done. However, they do have their shortcomings. For starters, they are mechanical, therefore they require adjustment, and there will be wearing over time. Excessive wear or poor adjustment will eventually have an adverse affect on the timing

Proper Gears and Mesh

How the distributor is driven is important to its accuracy and longevity. Camshafts are made of different blends of metals and materials, so the distributor gear must be made of compatible metallurgical materials. Generally, the distributor gear is made of a slightly softer metal so if there is a failure, the distributor gear will take the brunt of the destruction, simply because it is less expensive and easier to replace.

As for which gear is right for your engine, it depends on the camshaft. It is best to contact the cam manufacturer for a recommendation, but here are some tips as a rule-of-thumb. An iron gear, which most distributors are supplied with, is the choice for flat-tappet camshafts, which is the most common cam. If you have a roller camshaft, most common in racing and very high-performance engines, a bronze gear will be required.

Throughout the 1990s, hydraulic roller camshafts were used in a lot of OEM engines and these cams are still lifting the valves in many of their crate motors. Most of these camshafts will require a special distributor gear made of a steel material. A prime example is the Ford 302 of the late 1980s through the mid 1990s, which comes with a hydraulic roller cam and thus requires a steel gear.

Another gear aspect is the mesh between the two gears. If the gears are not meshing properly, the timing will not be absolutely accurate. This is more of a concern on high-end race engines such as those built for NASCAR. MSD offers oversized bronze gears for several of their racing distributors. The gears are oversized from 0.003 to 0.015 inch for Chevrolet applications.

Gear material is an important choice that depends on the camshaft of your engine. Different core materials are used in a variety of cam applications, and you need to make sure you have the correct distributor gear to match the camshaft. Most distributors are supplied with iron gears. However, hydraulic roller cams require a special steel gear and racing roller cams will require a bronze gear.

Engineers at MSD designed this distributor-to-cam gear fixture so they could study the differences in gear mesh. You can see the way the helical gears mesh together. By using an oversized distributor gear, any slop in the gear mesh will be removed, resulting in more accurate timing. This is overkill for most street engines, but many top-level race teams look at these minute details.

Excessive endplay of a stock distributor can be tightened by installing shims between the housing and the gear. Moroso offers distributor shims for a couple different applications. This can also help set the position of the distributor gear farther down if there is a mesh problem with the cam gear. A stock Chevrolet cast distributor may have endplay measuring anywhere from 0.013 - 0.030 inch, and you wouldn't want to go much less than 0.005 inch (unless you're working with a precision built aftermarket distributor).

nd quality of the spark. Another point s that they were designed to handle a mall amount of current, which limits heir potential output. Also, points end to bounce at higher racing RPM, esulting in the points burning and the gnition missing.

The adjustment that we just mentioned is termed setting the dwell. The dwell time is measured in the number of degrees of the distributor's rotation that the contacts of the points are closed. This is the time frame is called coil saturation time. Coil saturation

time is the time that the coil has to produce a strong magnetic field to create a high-voltage spark to fire across the spark plug gap. If the points open too much, the dwell time is reduced, so the voltage output of the coil will be weak. This could cause a misfire under loads.

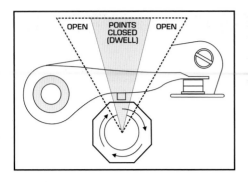

This diagram shows the operation of the points. When they are closed, the coil is building up current in its primary windings. When the points open, this field collapses to the secondary windings, creating a high-voltage spark that is delivered to the distributor and spark plug wires. Notice that opening the points too much will diminish the dwell.

One answer to insufficient coil saturation time from points is the dual-point distributor from Mallory. Each set is precisely positioned with one being slightly staggered. In this setup, the first set is just closing as the second set is opening. The result is increased dwell time over a single point system.

If the dwell time is too long (the gap doesn't open as much), then an arc may occur across the contact points resulting in failure of the points, as well as poor coil output.

Another important component within a points system is the condenser. The condenser is behind the scenes, but an important part of the breaker-point system. When the contact points open the condenser, ensures a clean break of

Adjusting and Setting Points

When adjusting the points gap on the bench, a new set should be opened slightly more than a used set. A new set should be opened to around .018 – .020 inch, while a used set could be about .014 -.017 inch. The new points are set a touch wider to accommodate for the rubbing block to seat into to the distributor cam. This should only be to get the gap close, as the dwell should be checked and adjusted with engine running using a dwell meter.

People that have a dwell meter, and know how to use it, are becoming scarce. A dwell meter simply connects to 12 volts and ground from the battery, then has a lead that connects to the negative terminal of the coil. Here we see the dwell set at approximately 32° — perfect!

As a rule of thumb, the dwell should be set between 28° - 32°. It can be adjusted through the window of the distributor cap by moving the Allenhead screw that adjusts the position of the breaker arm.

the current flow. This causes the current to move out of the coil rather than across the points gap. If the condenser is faulty, the points will show premature and excessive burning. If the condenser were shorted, it would cause a no-start condition. It is rare that a condenser ever fails or causes trouble, so you don't hear too much about it, but it is an important part of the breaker point system.

ELECTRONIC TRIGGERS

In the early 1970s, electronic triggers were creeping into OEM distributors. Chrysler got there and Ford soon followed. They both opted to use a magnetic pickup in their distributors. The first mass-produced electronic distributor from the halls of General Motors was the High Energy Ignition

(HEI) unitized distributor, which wa in every GM product by 1975. No only did this distributor incorporate magnetic pickup design but it also ha the coil incorporated into its cap Though the distributor was considerably bulky, it offered a single wire hook-up and there was no other external components or wiring. These benefits have kept the GM HEI extremely popular among enthusiasts, and they are still widely used and are even supplied in many of the General's curren crate engines. There are also many companies, such as Performance Distributors, that offer performance modules and components to update origina models.

Over the years, the ignition module of the GM HEI distributor wen through several reiterations with th ignition module. The ignition modul

The GM HEI distributor is still a popular choice for many enthusiasts, thanks to its one-wire installation and internal coil. In fact, they're popular enough that Davis Unified Incorporated offers them to fit Ford and Chrysler engines in a variety of performance levels.

MSD Pickup Polarity

If you are running an MSD Ignition control with a magnetic pickup and you are not sure about the polarity, you can connect the wires one way and check the timing of the engine. Next, swap the position of the wires and check the timing again. You'll notice that the timing changes significantly and may appear very erratic. When used with an analog controlled ignition control, such as their 6AL, the correct connection is when the timing is most retarded. However, if you're using a digitally controlled MSD, the correct polarity connection is when the timing is advanced. The difference is due to differences of the input circuit used in the two ignitions. Depending on the brand of distributor or ignition you are using, you should check with their tech line for polarity and ignition compatibility.

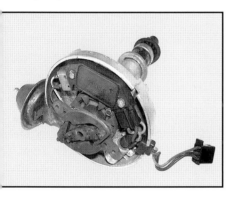

The inside of an HEI distributor doesn't look much different than a points distributor. There is still a mechanical advance, a vacuum canister, and even a condenser. Note that the diameter of the distributor is much wider.

A magnetic pickup is a compact and simple device. They're very accurate, reliable and will never require adjustment. They do require some sort of electronic device to control the flow of voltage and current through the coil.

is responsible for controlling the dwell time and the switching of the high voltage. The first versions used a module with four terminals, had a centrifugal advance, and a vacuum canister. The aftermarket primarily offers four-pin modules. As more electronics made their way into cars, the HEI eventually lost the vacuum canister. These distributors used a module with seven terminals. For a short while, there was also a five-pin module that had very limited timing controls, so there was still vacuum advance. Throughout these different styles, the same style pickup was used, as well as the mechanical advance.

MAGNETIC AND HALL-EFFECT PICKUPS

The use of an electronic ignition trigger has many benefits. There is, of course, the absence of mechanically moving components, which means that there are no adjustments or parts to wear. Also, breaker points are limited to the amount of primary current that can be used, while electronically triggered ignitions can work with higher amperage and voltage. This means that electronically triggered ignitions will produce higher secondary output! For the end user, this means a hotter spark to help improve combustion, equating to increased power.

Electronic triggers are only responsible for producing a trigger signal. Whether it be a magnetic pickup or a Hall-effect switch, there still must be an ignition module of some sort that controls the dwell time. This is accomplished through different methods such as with a small module inside the distributor, like in a GM HEI distributor, or with an external box like a Ford Duraspark or Chrysler system. Note that these methods are all inductive ignition systems. They use electronic circuitry and engine RPM to derive predetermined dwell times. There are several types of electronic pickups used in distributors. They share common traits and do complete the same task, but they go about this task in different ways.

Magnetic Pickup

When electronic ignitions replaced breaker points, magnetic pickups were the choice of most OEMs due to their reliability and accuracy. There are only two wires to connect and they are very reliable because of their simple construction. This is probably why they're the most popular form of electronic trigger.

The magnetic pickup consists of a magnet that has a small wire wound around it to create a magnetic field, similar to an ignition coil. This pickup is mounted into a trigger plate on the base of the distributor. A metal trigger wheel, generally referred to as a reluctor, is mounted to the distributor shaft. The reluctor has a tab or paddle for

PICKUP	POLARITY POSITIVE	POLARITY NEGATIVE
MSD Distributor	Black/Orange	Black/Violet
Accell 46/4800 Series	Black/Orange	Black/Violet
Accell 51/6100 Series	Red	Black
Chrysler Distributor	White/Orange	Black
Ford Distributor	Black/Orange	Black/Violet
GM Distributor	White	Green
MSD Ignition Control	Violet	Green
Moroso Crank Trigger Pickup	White	Black
MSD Crank Trigger Pickup	Violet	Green
Mallory Crank Trigger Pickup	Violet	Green
Hayes Stinger	Black/Green	Black

This chart shows the polarity of several common magnetic pickups. If the wires are connected backwards, the ignition timing will be inconsistent and the engine will run rough. Depending on what kind of ignition control you use, the timing may appear retarded or advanced as well.

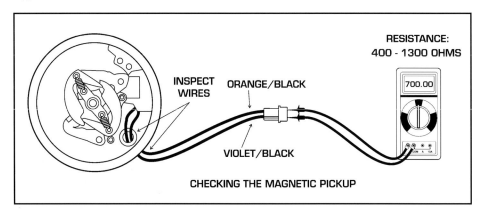

CHECKING THE MAGNETIC PICKUP

Magnetic Pickup Wiring

Routing the magnetic pickup wires can be very important to your engine's performance. Since a magnetic pickup produces a voltage signal to trigger the ignition, it is important that the wires are routed away from other wiring, electrical components, the primary coil leads, and spark plug wires. This will help prevent chances of interference that could cause a false, or erratic trigger signal. This is especially important in today's performance world with aftermarket EFI systems, electric water pumps, and more.

Magnetic pickup wires should be twisted together to help create a field around the wires for protection. Also try to route the pickup wiring as close as possible to the engine block, frame, or chassis of the car. These parts serve as large ground planes, so there is less electrical activity near their surface. For the ultimate protection, you can make a shielded harness that provides a grounded shield around the wires. MSD offers a six-foot shielded harness, PN 8862, which is recommended on high-performance applications, especially with EFI.

Checking the resistance of your distributor's magnetic pickup is about the only form of troubleshooting you can do without an oscilloscope. The resistance of a Mallory, MSD, or Holley magnetic pickup should be between 400 – 1,300 ohms. Be sure to check the connections for a tight, clean fit. Most Problems are due to poor connections or crimp troubles.

each cylinder and spins past the stationary magnetic pickup. Every time one of these paddles passes the pickup assembly, a voltage signal is created that is used to trigger the coil or ignition. As the edge of the paddle lines up with the pickup, a negative voltage is made. When the paddle passes through the signal, the voltage signal becomes a positive voltage. This voltage output increases with the RPM of the engine, making it very reliable and less susceptible to electronic interference.

The two wires of a magnetic pickup have polarity, so they can only be connected one way. This makes it important to know which wire is positive and which is negative. The chart shows some common pickups and their polarity.

When troubleshooting a no-start condition you can also check the resistance of the pickup. It is very rare for a magnetic pickup to fail, because of their simple construction and lack of moving components. However, stranger things have happened.

Hall-Effect Pickup

A Hall-effect switch is similar to a magnetic pickup, though instead of creating its own voltage to use as a trigger signal, it receives constant power from a positive voltage source (usually a 12 volt source). A magnet is used to lower (turn off) or raise (turn on) this voltage to produce a trigger signal. This system creates a square wave signal that remains at the same amplitude throughout the RPM range of the engine.

There are different ways of accomplishing the switching feat with a Hall-effect pickup design. Typically, the Hall-effect switch is mounted inside the distributor, on the outer edge of the housing, while a magnet is permanently mounted just inside the switch to create a magnetic field. Like the reluctor used with the magnetic pickup, a Hall-effect device incorporates a shutter wheel that either opens or blocks the magnetic field between the pickup and magnet. When the two are blocked off, there is no magnetic field, which means the switch is turned off. When the window

What's the Point?

We may have mentioned their bad points, but there are cases when you can keep your points, or at least your numbers-matching distributor, and still improve the performance of your ignition. Not every car needs a billet aluminum distributor, and for a weekend cruiser or something that isn't revved up to redline constantly, you can get by on a good working, accurate distributor.

It is true, that a magnetic pickup distributor is much more accurate than a points distributor, especially when it is complemented with an adjustable advance, sealed bearings, and a billet housing.

In order to accomplish this, you need to make sure that the distributor is in good working order. That is, the

You can easily upgrade your stock points distributor to an electronic trigger with a kit from Pertronix. A Hall-effect switch mounts in place of the breaker points and a ring with eight magnets installs under the mechanical advance plate. Pertronix has the most applications available for these points-to-electronics kits.

bushings are solid and there is no wobble or excessive end play. Also, the mechanical advance should be in accurate working order and set-up properly for your engine. While you're at it, you may want to check out the vacuum advance as well.

Okay, so the distributor checks out okay, then what are your options? If you just can't handle the thought of having age-old breaker-point technology under the distributor cap, you can easily replace them with an electronic trigger kit such as those offered by Pertronix or Crane.

Pertronix offers the Ignitor and Ignitor II kits that provide an easy way to install a Hall-effect type pickup as an alternative to points. The Ignitor kits feature a thin reluctor wheel that has a magnet for each cylinder. This reluctor installs on the bottom of the advance plate, just beneath the rotor. The points assembly and condenser are removed and replaced with a Hall-effect-style pickup.

Two wires come from the Ignitor pickup and connect to the coil positive terminal (where it receives 12 volts), and the coil negative terminal. Just like that, you have an electronic ignition that produces more voltage than the points ever did, plus it is maintenance free! The upgraded Ignitor II actually produces even more energy and voltage, so you receive the benefits of a hotter spark as well as never having to adjust the points again!

Crane recently introduced an electronic module that simply replaces the points. It uses the stock cam on the distributor to produce its trigger signal. The unit is digitally controlled and is almost too simple to install. An even tricker feature of this module is a built-in rev limiter! You can get rid of the points in your restored muscle car and have the protection of an over-rev limiter as well.

The final option is to bite the breaker-points bullet by realizing that you never zing the engine into points float to begin with. You can easily wire in a CD ignition control like a 6-Series from Crane, Mallory, or MSD and use the points to trigger it. You'll get all the benefits of the high-energy multiple sparks plus the points will probably never need to be replaced again. For more information, go back and take a look at Chapter 2.

Crane recently introduced its XR-i points replacement kit that simply bolts in place of the points and uses the original cam wheel. An added bonus is that it has a built-in adjustable rev limiter.

of the wheel passes through the magnet and sensor becomes aligned again, it creates a field to turn the switch on.

Like the reluctor, the shutter wheel of a Hall-effect system will have eight openings and closings for each cylinder (six for a 6-cylinder, four on 4-cylinders). The benefit of this trigger system is that it produces a constant voltage signal output, since the device is turned on and off, rather than switching from a negative to a positive voltage. A Hall-

Hall-effect switches were used in Ford's TFI distributors from the late 1980s and into the 1990s. The Ford design incorporated a stationary magnet. The magnet signal is interrupted by a shudder wheel that blocks the magnetic field turning the switch off. Once it passes, the switch is turned on again by the recurring magnetic field.

Mallory offers a variety of distributors with breaker points, magnetic pickups, and optical trigger devices. Their popular Unilite distributors use a photo coupler that receives a beam of infrared light from their module. A shutter wheel breaks the light beam, producing the trigger signal telling electronic circuitry to fire the stored energy from the coil. This example carries two Unilite modules to incorporate a redundant ignition system. Such a setup is popular in circle track racing.

effect switch is very accurate, though they cost a little more than a magnetic pickup, plus there's an extra power wire to connect.

Optical Pickup

An optical pickup or photo-optic system is a well-known electronic trigger device. This type of trigger device is a derivative of a Hall-effect switch, since it also incorporates a shutter wheel that essentially turns the switch on and off. The difference is that instead of a magnetic field being sensed, it uses an infrared LED.

Inside the distributor housing, a light sensing receptor is mounted directly across from a small LED that produces the light. The openings and closings of the shudder wheel break the light beam to the receptor, which produces the trigger signal for the self-contained electronic control.

Like a Hall-effect switch, an optical trigger requires a three-wire installation, including a 12-volt source for the electronic control, a ground, and a trigger wire to the negative terminal on the coil. Most optically triggered ignitions can be used as a stand-alone distributor, or they can be used to trigger an external ignition control, such as a Mallory Hyfire ignition.

MECHANICAL ADVANCE

As if the distributor doesn't have enough responsibilities, it also must match the ignition timing to the ever-changing requirements of the engine. This is an important job, because an engine's timing requirements change as RPM increases. The following chapter will delve into more detail on ignition timing and the available controls, so we will keep this explanation brief to get an understanding of the distributor's timing advance mechanism.

At idle, a spark occurs on a piston's compression stroke a few degrees before it reaches top dead center (TDC). At this point, the air/fuel mixture is ignited beginning the combustion process. The act of combustion remains a constant for the most part, but when the piston is traveling at a much higher speed, the initiation of the combustion process must occur sooner.

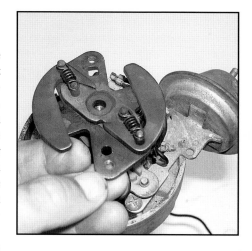

The operation of a centrifugal advance assembly is simple, yet very important to your engine's performance. As the distributor spins, the weights overcome the tension of the springs and push out from the center of the distributor. This advances the trigger function of the distributor. Note the worn pads where the weights swing on this old points distributor.

The advance assembly is mounted on top of distributor shaft on all of MSD's models, even this Ford distributor. This makes it very easy to change the advance springs to alter the rate of advance. There is also a stop bushing under the advance plate that can be replaced to control the amount of advance that occurs. This way you have better control and the ability to make easier total-timing adjustments.

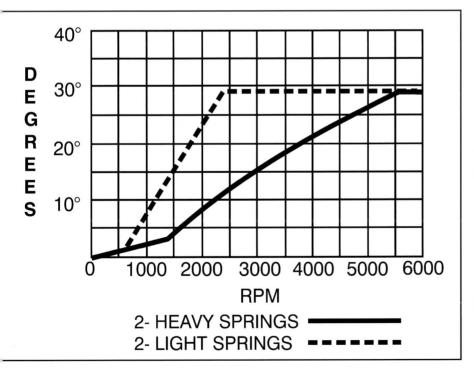

This chart shows the variety of timing curves you can achieve simply by changing the advance springs on the distributor. Moroso offers an advance kit for GM distributors. Different tension springs control new weights designed for smooth movement to eliminate erratic timing.

Therefore the spark must occur more advanced in the compression stroke to obtain the best combustion and results on the power stroke. To meet these demands, distributors are equipped with an advance mechanism that operates through centrifugal force.

This mechanical advance assembly is made up of two weights that are pushed out by the spinning force of the distributor. Springs are attached to the weights to control the rate at which they extend. The weights are mounted on an advance plate and there are generally some sort of pads that the weights slide on for smooth timing changes. There is also some manner of a stop bushing so the total amount of advance can be controlled. This assembly is attached to the trigger assembly of the distributor so it moves forward resulting in the ignition being triggered earlier (advanced).

By swapping different tension springs, you can alter how quickly the timing advances. A spring with less tension lets the weight spin out easier to advance the timing quickly. Many companies offer advance kits that consist of different weights and springs to fit a variety of distributors so you can dial-in an advance curve to match your engine's needs.

The mechanical advance is an important element in tuning your engine. A slow advance can hinder performance, while too much advance can cause pre-ignition resulting a loss of power or even engine damage. This is why it is important to check the timing at idle and at higher RPM so you know what the total advance is set at.

VACUUM ADVANCE

Vacuum-advance canisters were used primarily as a way to increase the engine's fuel economy. The canister provides a way to advance the ignition timing during moderate and part-throttle conditions. This is when the load on the engine is lower and vacuum is higher. The canister has a diaphragm with a mechanical link that is connected to the pickup plate in the distributor. When vacuum is applied, the pickup plate is pulled, which

Most vacuum advance canisters use a ported vacuum source that is above the throttle plates on a carburetor. This way, there is only advance when the throttle blades are open.

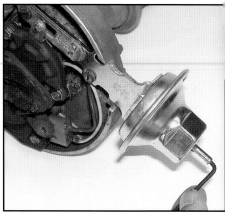

Moroso offers an adjustable vacuum canister for GM's HEI, internal-coil distributor. There is an adjustment screw inside the canister that allows you to set the amount of advance it will supply.

CAPS AND ROTORS

The distributor cap and rotor are part of the secondary side of the ignition, meaning they are components that receive the high voltage from the coil. These components are important to trouble-free performance and should be inspected and replaced periodically. How often really depends on how often you drive your car and even where you live. Areas that exhibit a lot of humidity and changes in temperature will cause more corrosion to occur in the cap. When an engine is run, the air within the cap obviously heats up, and then cools again when the engine is shut off. This can cause condensation to occur, which will cause the brass terminals of a cap to corrode. Racers and other performance enthusiasts will sometimes drill a few holes in the cap to help vent the air.

The rotor and cap on a race engine should be inspected as routine maintenance between events. Check inside the cap for signs of carbon tracking, which is the fingerprint of spark scatter. This will appear as a small jagged line that looks like someone drew it with a pencil. Check the tightness of the rotor screws and inspect the rotor tip for signs of pitting or wear, especially on the end. High-output ignitions can put a lot of heat across the rotor tip, so keep an eye on it. Also, sparks like to leave from a nice sharp edge to cross over to

advances when the trigger signal is created. Vacuum drops when the engine is accelerated, so the advance turns off to prevent detonation from occurring.

In most cases, the vacuum source for the advance canister is located above the carburetor's throttle plates. This is called ported vacuum, as opposed to manifold vacuum, which is when an inlet is connected directly to the intake manifold. The difference here is that

manifold vacuum is there constantly. The ported source provides vacuum only when the throttle blades are open, which is the way most vacuum advance systems are connected.

The amount of advance that occurs varies, but it generally ranges from 10 – 15°. Some companies offer an adjustable vacuum-advance canister. This lets you set the exact amount of vacuum advance that your engine requires.

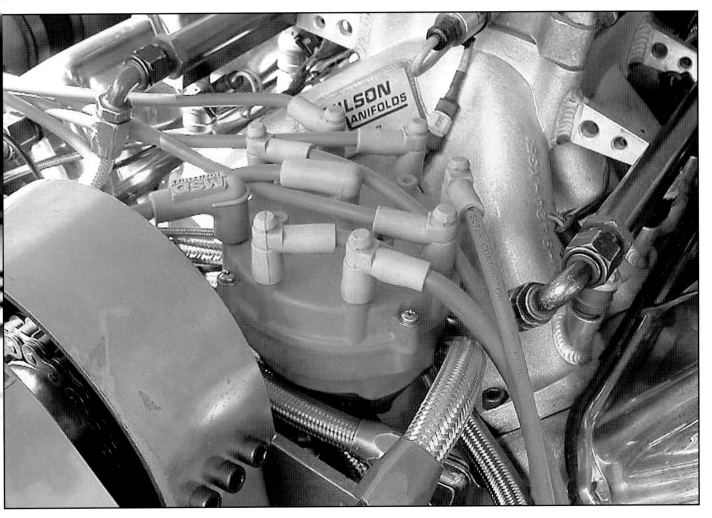

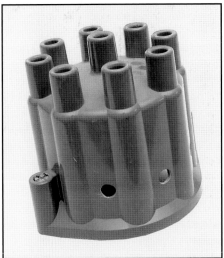

MSD offers a Cap-A-Dapt kit that gives you the ability to install a larger distributor cap and rotor. They have kits available for most of their applications, like this huge Pro-Cap version.

the plug wire terminal, so if the rotor tip is rounded from wear, it's time replace it. Don't scrimp on an OEM-type rotor if a better aftermarket one is available for your application. Stock parts are made from an easy-to-break plastic and most will only have the tip pressed in place. Look for a rotor with a rotor tip that is screwed down to offer improved strength and durability.

Size Helps

There's a lot of electrical activity going on inside the confines of the distributor cap. Consider the rotor receiving eight spark pulses and delivering them to eight different posts within one rotation! All of these sparks also mix with the stagnate air inside the cap to form a gas called ozone which can be slightly conductive. This is not something you want to occur within the cap.

When choosing a distributor for a high-performance engine, try to go with the largest cap and rotor you can fit for your application. This is less important in mild street applications, as they're at cruising and moderate throttle with low load most of the time. On a race car that is at all or nothing, the bigger the cap, the better. By increasing the diameter of the cap, there is more room inside the cap and the terminals are spaced farther apart to ensure that the spark gets the right terminal at the correct time. Of course, there are situations that simply do not allow for a large distributor cap. When this is the case, the cap and rotor need to be high on the inspection list between runs.

In high-humidity areas, drilling a few holes in the distributor cap will help vent the ozone gases that can build up inside smaller distributor caps. The holes should be beneath the rotor skirt and about 3/8-in diameter. This cap is supplied pre-drilled from MSD.

DISTRIBUTORS AND TIMING
Dialing in Centrifugal Advance

Now that we've gone over some of the basic operation of the distributor and timing, we'll delve into their aspects a little closer. First though, you need to consider your application and what you need out of a distributor.

Obviously, there are a lot of different distributors available in the viable aftermarket, or what about rebuilding your own? Cost is of obvious concern, and not all engines are going to require a top-end distributor. One thing to watch out for are the extremely inexpensive replacement distributors. Remember, you get what you pay for. And don't forget that the distributor is responsible for driving your engine's oil pump as well as controlling the timing. Don't be drawn in by cast aluminum distributors that have been polished smooth so they appear to be billet. Also, for these distributors to be as low-priced as they are, there must be some corners being cut in the quality. In short, be aware of what you're buying, and the company that built it.

If you're rebuilding an engine for your muscle car and it is going to be mostly a stock engine, you may even consider sticking with the stock distributor. If you chose this route, it is important to make sure the distributor is in good mechanical working condition. That is, the shaft doesn't wobble, the gear is in good condition, and the

There are a lot of distributors to choose from when you're putting together a performance ignition system. Having a plan as to your engine's intended use and performance goals will lead you to the right distributor set up.

advance assembly moves freely and returns to its idle position. Once the mechanicals are in good working order, you can decide what you want to use as a trigger for the ignition, or if you want to add a high-output ignition to

improve its driveability. Of course, an electronic replacement kit like those we mentioned in Chapter 6 from Pertronix, Crane, or Mallory are all good upgrades over breaker points. If your engine uses a little oil or runs a touch rough at lower RPM, think about installing a hotter ignition module or stepping up to a multiple sparking ignition control. The multiple sparks really help burn rich air/fuel mixtures, and you can retain the stock distributor for appearance if you mount the control box in an inconspicuous location.

If you're putting together a good performing drivetrain and plan on taking advantage of this power with a heavy left foot, a new high-quality distributor should be in your future. Inaccurate triggering, poor timing advance, shaft wobble, or slop in the gear mesh will all rob your engine of power. The benefits of a stout new housing with fresh bearings or bushings, and a smooth mechanical advance that is adjustable are nice features that will prove themselves worth the investment in a short amount of time.

There are still options to consider. What style pickup seems to work best? Do you need vacuum advance for your engine? Do you have room for a large HEI-style distributor with the internal coil? Has your engine been decked or machined, or is it a tall-deck block that would require a special housing? Also, how much clearance does your intake combination or firewall allow? Many street rods or midsize pony cars don't have much in the way of room, which can limit your distributor selection. The aftermarket offers a variety of models some with small diameter housings for just such a case.

Timing Changes

One of the most important features of a distributor is the centrifugal advance. When you step up to a new distributor, be sure to pick something with an adjustable mechanical advance. Having the ability to match a timing curve to your engine's needs will help make sure you're getting all the performance possible from your engine.

The tricky thing about ignition timing is that one setting is just not ideal for the variety of different conditions an engine goes through. When it comes to achieving optimum torque and horsepower throughout the entire RPM range, the ignition timing curve is

Remember to think about the clearance in your engine compartment when choosing a distributor! This '65 Pontiac Tri-Power setup wouldn't allow a GM HEI distributor to fit due to the intake and rear carb. This would lead the owner to look at stock rebuilt distributors or other aftermarket models.

What's the Deal With Vacuum Advance?

The vacuum advance canister that you see hanging off the side of many distributors is another form of advancing the timing, but it does not really play a performance role.

Vacuum canisters were introduced to improve economy during times of high vacuum, such as at idle and moderate cruising speeds. The advance only happens under these conditions, and once you accelerate, vacuum drops and the timing returns to the mechanical amount. So you can see why they're not important to race engines.

Some engine builders have noted that a big cubic-inch engine, such as an Oldsmobile or Pontiac 455, will actually run a little cooler on long moderate drives when it is equipped with a vacuum advance.

A vacuum advance canister will generally up the timing by 10° – 15°. You can also get vacuum canisters that allow you to adjust the amount of advance, such as from Moroso. For the most part, vacuum advance works as an economy boosting tool and isn't required on performance applications.

No Boxes Please

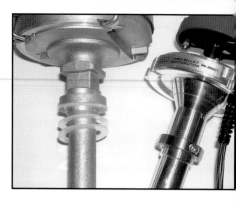

Many aftermarket distributors require an external ignition box. Most of MSD's Pro-Billet distributors require a CD ignition control such as a 6AL. There are certainly performance benefits of running the external ignition, but some people prefer or simply don't have the real estate to mount an external ignition control.

In these cases, Accel, Mallory, and MSD offer distributors that are ready-to-go. MSD's Ready-to-Run distributors use a magnetic pickup and have an inductive ignition module, much like a GM HEI, built into their housings to control the sparking chores. This ignition produces a high-powered spark but does not deliver multiple sparks like their other ignitions do. These dis-

tributors are a good choice for street rods that lack room for mounting extra parts, plus offer a clean installation. The Ready-to-Run distributor from MSD has three wires versus the two wires of their standard distributors.

Mallory offers a variety of distributors that are stand-alone models as well. Accel offers their BilletProof distributors with an even smaller housing that fits in tight engine compartments. These models both produce a high-output spark to improve performance through better combustion. Mallory and Accel both offer replacement points distributors that will drop right in and fire the coil with improved advance assemblies and features as well.

The magnetic pickup connector on the left is from an MSD distributor and requires an ignition box like their 6A series. The connector to the right is an MSD Ready-to-Run distributor, which does not require an external box. The three wires connect to ground, coil positive, and coil negative.

If your engine block or heads have been decked, or if you're running a special block with a raised cam, you may need to shim the distributor housing or get one with an adjustable slip collar. This will allow you to compensate for the different height of the mounting surface of the intake manifold. Moroso offers a pack of shims to make up for the difference.

imperative. The timing that you need during cranking and at an idle is not sufficient for high-RPM operation. Conversely, ideal high-RPM timing is not going to go over well during cranking or low speed operation. As RPM increases, the engine requires different ignition timing due to a list of changes that occur to the air/fuel mixture entering the cylinder. The main reason is the reduction in time that the mixture has to completely combust before the piston reaches top dead center (TDC) due to its increased speed.

Matching the spark with the piston's changing speed and position before top dead center (TDC) is necessary to achieve the most force possible on the piston. The combustion event of the air/fuel mixture itself remains a constant for the most part, but the change in piston speed affects when the spark must occur. At higher RPM, the piston travels through the compression stroke much quicker than at an idle, therefore, the spark must occur sooner to accomplish combustion ideally.

There are also many other variables that affect ignition timing. Fuel quality, combustion chamber design, intake combinations, cam specifications, and many more all need to be taken into consideration when setting the timing. For instance, a cam with a big profile

FACTOR	ADVANCE TIMING FOR	RETARD TIMING FOR
Cylinder Pressure	Low	High
Vacuum	High	Low
Energy of Ignition	Low	High
Fuel Octane	High	Low
Mixture (Air/Fuel)	Rich	Lean
Temperature	Cool	Hot
Combustion Chamber Shape	Open	Compact
Spark Plug Location	Offset	Center
Combustion Turbulence	Low	High
Load	Light	Heavy

These statistics all need to be considered when you're looking for the optimum timing setting for your application. Many engine shops or manufacturers will be able to point you in the right direction when setting the timing. Testing and tuning are the best tools you can use.

that improves breathing efficiency at top end will need more timing advance at low RPM. If then engine has been worked over to improve its breathing efficiency and has a higher compression ratio, less overall timing will be required. Other aspects of the engine and application that affect timing are shown in the chart.

Changes in the ignition timing are not limited to high-performance and race cars. Essentially anything that has ever rolled off an OEM assembly line required timing changes. Before modern computer controls handled the timing chores, engineers took advantage of centrifugal force by using a mechanical advance system inside the distributor to alter the timing as RPM increased. Sure, there hasn't been a new car with a distributor and centrifugal advance in almost two decades, but most of the engines being built for the street or mild strip use are still using this method with fine results. Before getting into setting up a distributor or checking the timing, there are a couple definitions to clarify.

Initial Timing: This refers to the timing when the engine is at an idle, which makes sense, since it is sometimes called the idle timing. This is also where the distributor happens to be positioned mechanically in the engine.

Centrifugal Advance: This is the curve that occurs to advance the timing as RPM increases. There are generally two parts to the centrifugal (or mechanical) advance, including the rate that the timing advances, as well as the point the advance stops.

Total Timing: This is the final point that the timing is able to reach. For instance, if you have the initial timing set at 8° with an advance curve limited to 26°, the total timing would be 34°. Just how quickly this point is reached depends on the RPM, acceleration, and the chosen rate of advance.

Now, we'll see how this all comes together.

CENTRIFUGAL ADVANCE

Centrifugal- or mechanical-advance assemblies consist of two weights that

Where's the Improvement?

So you just installed a new trick distributor, and after setting the timing, you head out for a test spin. The engine sounds fine but it just seems a little doggy or isn't quite what you thought it would be like with the new distributor. Did you tweak the centrifugal advance to match your engine?

Most aftermarket distributors are equipped with slow-reacting (stiff) advance springs. The reason behind this thinking is to prevent detonation from occurring. If a new distributor were to be dropped in and cause an engine to rattle or worse yet cause damage due to detonation, it would be a bad deal for everyone involved. Having the slower advancing springs in place will prevent that from occurring, plus it should get everyone to thumb through the installation instructions to figure out how to modify the curve to match their engine's specs.

Notice the difference in thickness between the springs. The heavy springs on the left are installed from the factory. Chances are you'll be pulling those off and going for one of the lighter sets of springs to fire up your engine.

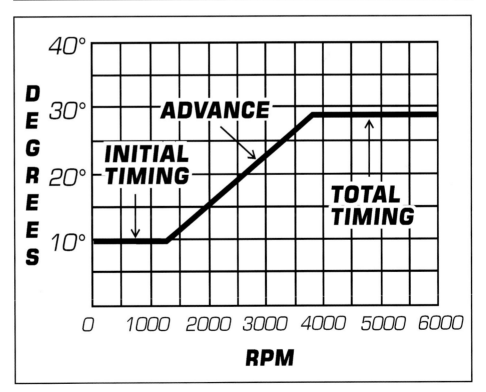

This chart shows a typical timing curve with the initial timing, the centrifugal advance, and the total timing.

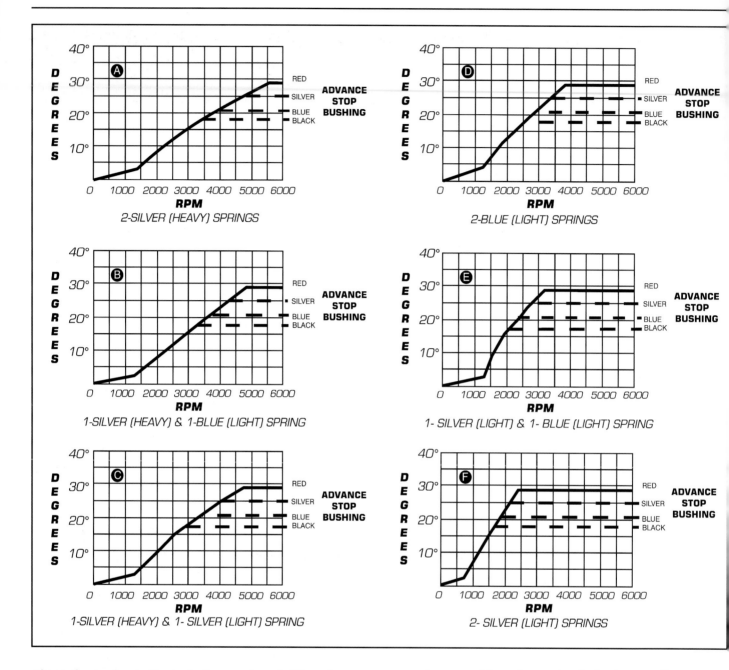

These charts clearly illustrate the number of different curves you can "program" into the mechanical advance. Changes are made by simply swapping three sets of advance springs and four stop bushings supplied with an MSD distributor.

These old distributor spin machines would allow you to spin your distributor and set up the advance, but finding one, or someone who knows how to use one, is getting tougher. Companies that specialize in distributors such as Davis Unified Incorporated will take note of your engine's specs and tune an advance curve to match your needs before sending it out the door.

are pushed out by the centrifugal force of the distributor. Have you ever been on one of those traveling circus rides that spins you around, then eventually the floor drops and yet you stay in the same position with your body firmly planted against the wall? If not, you're missing the first-hand effect of centrifugal force. Weights are connected to the advance plate that holds the trigger mechanism. As the weights get pushed out, the advance plate moves the pickup or pole piece opposite the rotation of

Installation/Removal

For some reason, people never seem to want to pull the distributor out of the engine. They do have a point in that yes, the timing will need to be checked and adjusted. But if you're replacing points or doing some maintenance on the advance, taking the distributor out of the engine will be worth the extra little bit of work, and it is actually very easy to do.

Start by removing the distributor cap. A few of the wires will probably need to be pulled off, so it is a good idea to mark all of the wires and their locations. With the cap off, you are going to need to rotate the engine until the rotor is pointing at a fixed mark. Either line it up with a bolt on the intake, straight ahead, or make a mark on the firewall. When you reinstall the distributor, the rotor must line back up at this point exactly, so it is important to have a mark that is easily identified. Another mark you can make is on the distributor housing and intake manifold. This will get the timing closer to your setting, but it isn't completely necessary.

Once everything is aligned and marked, loosen and remove the distributor hold-down clamp and move it out of the way. The distributor is now ready to be pulled out. Notice as you pull it out that the rotor turns slightly. This is due to the helical gear that meshes to the cam gear.

Before you reinstall the distributor, make sure the gasket or O-ring is in place on the housing. If you cleaned the distributor, it's never a bad idea to put some oil or grease on the distributor gear (this is absolutely required when installing a new distributor or gear!). Lower the distributor into the engine and make sure the rotor is in the vicinity of the mark you made. Remember, the helical gear will not allow the rotor tip to align until the distributor is fully seated. If the distributor just won't fully seat or align, chances are the oil pump shaft will need to be rotated. Most Fords you can simply wiggle a little and get the shaft to align. On Chevrolet engines, you may need to use a long, flat-blade screwdriver to turn the oil pump shaft a little and try again. The distributor will drop into position.

Once the distributor is in place with the rotor aligned, install the hold-down clamp and distributor cap. Then start the engine and adjust the timing.

If the engine has been turned over, or no marks were made, you will have to bring the engine up to top dead center on the number-1 cylinder. This can easily be done by removing the number-1 spark plug and turning the engine over with your thumb placed over the spark plug hole. When the cylinder is on the compression stroke, you'll feel the air being pushed out around your thumb. Also at this point, the timing indicator should be lining up with TDC on the balancer, and if a valve cover is off, you'll notice that the intake and exhaust valves are both closed.

You can install the distributor once TDC for the number-1 cylinder is located. Wherever the rotor is pointing, is going to be the number-1 plug firing. Install the cap and the wires, making sure to follow the engine's firing order.

Before removing the spark plug wires and distributor cap, always mark the spark plug wires, their location, and the firing order of the engine. This will save you a lot of hassles, and possibly backfires, when re-installing everything again.

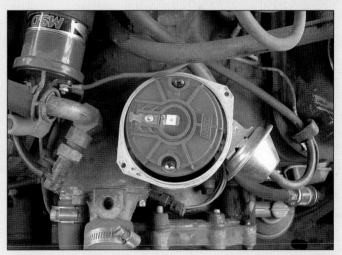

Turn the engine over until the rotor is facing an easy to align mark. This could be something on the firewall, engine, or simply a point straight ahead. In our case, we aimed it right at the the heater tube. When you lift the distributor out, note that it rotates a little due to the cut of the gears. Take that into consideration when you're installing it again.

Finding the timing indicators can sometimes be a hassle. There's more to setting the ignition timing than simply turning the distributor and lining up timing marks. Don't forget about mechanical advance and total timing!

A good timing light is imperative when you're tuning your ignition timing, and there are many to choose from. Also, having a degreed balancer or a timing tape and a clean, easy-to-view indicator are just as important.

Timing lights with removable leads lend themselves to a tidy storage. But more importantly, if they ever get caught in the fan, you won't be out an entire light. The damage will be limited to the harness (hopefully not a radiator too) that can be replaced for a few bucks.

the distributor. The result of this is that it triggers the ignition sooner.

The weights of the advance assembly also have small springs attached that control how fast the weights are pushed out. The centrifugal force from the engine RPM has to overcome the force of the springs. Therefore, the springs control how quickly the timing is advanced. A heavy spring will require higher RPM, resulting in a slow advance. Lightweight springs allow the centrifugal advance to occur quickly. Generally, a quick advance rate is going to help most applications. Many companies such as Moroso or Mallory offer kits with different advance weights and springs so you can dial-in a timing curve to your stock distributor.

Some aftermarket distributors also have a replaceable stop bushing that gives you the ability to limit the total amount of advance that occurs. This is an important feature, as it allows you to limit the advance to keep your engine out of detonation at high RPM. An MSD distributor comes with four bushings that have different diameters to allow the advance plate to move a certain distance. This distance equates to the number of degrees that the timing will advance. The four bushings supplied allow for 18°, 21°, 25°, and 28° of advance.

CHECKING THE IGNITION TIMING

Accurately checking and adjusting the timing sounds easy enough, and it is, but there are a lot of things to take into consideration to ensure it is set accurately. The timing needs to be checked at an idle and as you accelerate, so you can see where the total timing is set. Also, do you have a degreed balancer so you can tell the total timing, or do you need a dial-back timing light? What about a timing tape or an easy-to-view indicator?

A good place to start is with the main tool you need to set the timing: a timing light. A timing light has an inductive pickup that clamps to the number-1 spark plug wire. When the spark travels through the plug wire, this pickup senses it making the strobe of the timing light flash to show the position of the timing indicator on the balancer. This is the same effect a strobe

Having a good quality distributor hold-down clamp is often overlooked. There are many clamps available that are thick, flex-free steel and have machined tips that grip the sleeve of the distributor. Some of these real beefy models may not work with stock-style cast housings, so be sure to ask the manufacturer.

...ight on a dance floor has when it seems to freeze you for a fraction of a moment as you're bustin' a move. Except it occurs much faster on the engine, and you won't be embarrassed by setting your timing correctly.

As with most tools, there are several versions of timing lights available, and they can range from fairly cheap to upwards of a couple hundred dollars. If you're shopping for a light, ask yourself what you're looking to accomplish along how much you can spend. If you're only going to be setting the timing occasionally on your street machine you may not need the double-throw-down digital dial-back timing light with a triple chrome housing and carbon-fiber carrying case. However, if your engine strives on dead-nuts accurate timing within a degree, stepping up to a better quality light could be beneficial.

Next to accuracy, one of the most important features is the brightness of the strobe. You need something with a very bright strobe that is easy to read even in bright daylight. Sometimes it's tough to even locate the timing pointer on an engine, so having a light that can easily brighten up the indicator and the degree marks will make timing tuning easier. Another thing to look for is a metal inductive pickup that clamps to the spark plug wire. A low quality plas-

Dial-Up Total Timing

Dial-back timing lights are helpful in checking the centrifugal advance and total timing, especially if your engine doesn't have a degreed balancer. These lights have a dial on the back of their housing that is marked off in degree increments. After checking and setting the initial timing, you can position this dial to your desired total timing. If you're shooting for 40° of total timing by 3,000 rpm, you simply set the dial on

40° and begin to rev up the engine. At first, you won't see the indicator on the balancer, because it will be 40° before top dead center (BTDC). As the RPM increases, the indicator on the balancer will become visible. If everything is set up properly, the indicator will align with the zero mark when your timing reaches 40°. This is a nice feature, in that you don't have to have a degreed balancer or timing tape.

This older dial-back timing light from Snap-On has a dial control that lets you select the total timing. When the centrifugal advance is completely in, the timing mark should align with zero. New lights are available with a digital readout.

A self-powered timing light will be helpful in applications where the battery has been relocated to the trunk, such as drag cars or street rods. They use internal batteries, so there are no wires to connect to power and ground. These are also ideal on race engines with magnetos since they don't have a battery.

The stock balancer on this Buick 455 only has a line that indicates TDC and a tab off the timing chain cover with a few hash marks for degrees. In this case a dial-back timing light is handy to help set total timing.

A numbered timing decal can be applied to the balancer to help set the timing more accurately. Be sure to clean off any grease or grime to get the tapes to stick well. Make sure to match the decal to the diameter of the balancer or the degree increments will be off.

Moroso has a few nifty clamps and timing indicator accessories. This assembly has a pointer and the distributor degrees are indicated, so you can adjust the timing accurately without ever getting the timing light out of the toolbox. The thickness of the degree bracket must be taken into consideration of the distributor's installed height to retain proper gear mesh and the connection to the intermediate shaft. Also, this is measured from the cam, so 2° is equal to 4° at the crankshaft.

With the degrees marked off on the balancer, all you need is a solid pointer to read the timing. There are aftermarket versions or you can simply fabricate one out of a steel wire length. Just make sure it is mounted solid and stays still.

tic pickup will inevitably meet with an exhaust header and you'll be stuck with a useless inductive blob. Metal pickups seem to be hard to come by, so at least make sure the pickup is a better quality plastic and it clamps or locks in place.

Another key aspect to a timing light is obviously its accuracy. This can be tough to pinpoint. The only real way to

test a light's accuracy is with advanced electronic equipment. Or, you can compare your light with a friend's light and another light. But which one is right?!

Get to Know Your Light

It is important to only use one light on your car. Never use one light at home or on the dyno and then swap to a different light at the track. It is also important to always use the same ignition system at the engine dyno and the track, as timing variances can occur between different ignition controls as well. Being consistent in the pits with the way you tune up and work on your car will lead to consistent performance on the track.

Indicators and Degrees

You can have the brightest, most accurate timing light available, but if you don't have a clear timing mark on the balancer or pointer, it's not going to do you any good. Like most any piece from the factory, the timing pointer is designed to be adequate at best, and it just wasn't intended for precise tuning

capabilities. Most are flimsy stamped pieces with hard to read numbers or even just notches. Stock balancers will just have a timing line stamped at the TDC point for the number one cylinder, so there's not much of a chance to check the total advance. This combination doesn't make for the most accurate way to set the ignition timing.

Most aftermarket balancers come with timing degrees marked off through 90° or can be fully degreed so you can view the timing of different cylinders if you desire. For those out there with stock components, you can add a timing tape to the balancer to help check the total timing. This is a perfect example of when a dial-back timing light would be nice. These tapes are matched to different diameter balancers and feature degreed increments to help with the timing.

Timing Tips

With your trusty timing light in hand, you're ready to get the distributor settled in place. Remember that the engine is going to be running and you'll even be revving the engine, so always make sure to take the necessary safety precautions.

Connect the inductive pickup to the number-1 plug wire as close to the spark plug as possible to result in a strong signal.

Make sure the wiring of the timing light does not get moved or pulled near moving components.

If you are adjusting the distributor with the engine running, try to grab the base of the distributor to make adjustments. If you have a high-output ignition providing the fire, you'll make a good ground source for the spark to run to. (In fact, maybe get a buddy to rotate the distributor while you watch the timing!)

After getting the initial timing positioned, tighten the distributor's hold-down clamp, then check the total timing by revving the engine upwards to 3,000 rpm. You'll see the timing mark advance. If the advance is not what you were thinking your total should be, you may need to adjust the centrifugal advance.

Some timing light inductive pickups are directional and must be connected in one certain way in order to get a correct reading.

EFI Timing

On early model cars with distributors and electronic fuel injection, such as the 5.0-liter Mustangs, the distributor doesn't have a centrifugal advance curve. Timing chores are handled by the ECU, and the distributor is simply locked out. You can still watch the timing change by revving the engine through the RPM range while using a timing light.

To check the timing on a Ford TFI (thick film integrated) equipped car, you need to find the 'spout' connector. This is generally found in the engine compartment near the distributor or on the passenger side wheel well. With the engine running, disconnect the connector to put the car in open-loop mode, which sets the timing at the initial point for adjustment. GM cars can be done similar to this routine, as there is a single brown and white wire that needs to be disconnected. Once the initial timing is adjusted, turn the engine off, reconnect the wiring, and go for a test drive.

On Fords with a TFI ignition system, the spout connector must be disconnected in order to accurately set the timing. Disconnecting this connector bypasses the timing input from the ECU so all that shows is initial timing.

The main benefit of moving to an aftermarket distributor on a later-model EFI car is for the strength and fresh tolerances. This Mallory distributor is a replacement for Ford TFI distributors. The billet housing is stronger than the cast original version, plus it is supplied with a better cap with retainer.

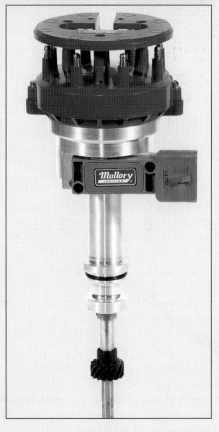

ELECTRONIC CONTROLS
Advanced Timing and Crank Triggers

So far, we've focused on the centrifugal and mechanical process of altering the ignition timing. This is by far the most popular manner of timing changes when it comes to street machines and mild performance applications. As with most anything mechanical, there are electronic alternatives. And there are a plethora of electronic timing controls for your ignition.

Electronic timing controls simply receive or intercept the trigger signal before the coil or ignition control to "pause" the signal through its circuitry resulting in retarding the timing. One thing to understand here is that there is no way for a timing control to advance the timing. A control cannot sense a trigger signal before the mag pickup or Hall-effect switch sends it. You still need to set the total timing with your distributor or a crank trigger and retard the timing from that point.

Being able to retard the timing is important in many cases, such as in times of detonation, when using nitrous, high boost pressures, or even simply at high RPM. Such systems can be beneficial in a number of applications, even when you still use centrifugal advance of the distributor. The variety of electronic timing controls ranges from a simple rheostat that retards the timing with the engine running, to a full-blown controller with cylinder-to-cylinder timing, multiple timing curves, retard stages, and more. Right now, we'll concentrate on a couple different versions that can come in handy for street cars.

MSD offers a timing control that has a dash mounted control knob so you can alter the timing as you drive down the road. There are different models that will connect to factory inductive ignition systems or an aftermarket CD ignition control such as a 6A. Originally, this was designed for tow vehicles that tugged the race trailer around. This way, if they encountered times of detonation from changes in

There are several timing controls available that make changing the timing as easy as turning the radio up. These controls are ideal for higher-compression engines that see a lot of street time.

Timing Controls –
More Than Just a Timing Retard

There is absolutely no way a timing control can advance the timing! These controls cannot see into the future and know when to trigger the ignition before the actual switching device does. But, there is a way to trick the system into thinking it can so you can achieve a sort of electronic advance.

When a timing control offers 15° of retard, you can split that to have 7° of advance with 8° of retard so you can have your cake and eat it too! Move the distributor to advance the timing the 7° and lock it in place. Then, fire up the engine and set the timing back to its original setting through the control knob. If your adjustment is correct, the dial should indicate 7°, and hocus-pocus, you can now advance the timing as well as retard it without even opening the hood. This can be helpful in a car that sees double duty as a daily driver and weekend warrior. For bracket cars, it saves you the hassle of having to move the distributor around.

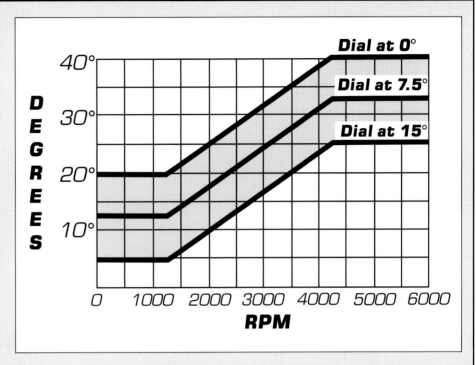

This chart shows how to cheat the timing control into thinking it can advance and retard the timing. By dividing the total amount of retard possible in half you can effectively have a timing advance and a timing retard at your fingertips.

altitude or poor quality gas, the timing could easily be retarded to dial away the detonation without even stopping. This is a much better alternative than stopping the truck and burning your knuckles to move the distributor! This setup can also be advantageous to performance applications.

If your street engine is on the verge of requiring high-octane gas, an adjustable timing control could be helpful. For daily or mild cruises you could simply retard the timing a few degrees by turning the control dial. When you're ready to get serious and hit the strip with some quality fuel, all you need to do is crank those few degrees right back in. You'll be ready to let 'er rip with a twist of the dial!

When using a timing control with a rheostat to change the timing manually, remember that the timing will be retarded across the entire ignition curve. This

includes the idle timing and the total timing after the centrifugal advance is all in. When you're just cruising at moderate throttle and the vacuum advance is active, the retard is also active. It's always there! What if you would rather have an amount of retard that is either on or off? There are plenty of options to step up to that will be covered in the following few pages. As we mentioned before, there are a lot of different electronic timing controls offered. It depends on your application and what you need out of the control. Perhaps you'd prefer to not to have any mechanical advance at all and let modern electronics take the responsibility? It can easily be done.

LOCKED-OUT

After spending two chapters discussing the benefits of the centrifugal

advance and trigger pickup of the distributor, we move to a chapter that negates both! But unlike high school literature classes, understanding the operation of the advance curve and the trigger pickup are something you will continue to use and consider as you work your way up the performance ladder.

There may come a point when your car is strictly for the race track or at least more strip than street. When this metamorphosis comes to fruition, there are certain things that you don't need to consider any more. Power steering or air conditioning? No thanks. Quiet exhaust and decent economy? Nope. Centrifugal advance? No thank you, just lock it out.

Now why would you want to lock out the centrifugal advance? Remember that as RPM changes, so do the engine's timing requirements. Daily driven cars

Got Boost? Need Retard

When the air and air/fuel mixture is being forced into the cylinder from a turbo or supercharger, the performance output of the engine jumps right up! That performance stems from increased cylinder pressures, which also change the timing requirements of the engine.

As boost pressure increases, so does the need for a timing retard. Crane and MSD offer ignition controls and add-on timing controls that allow you to retard the timing in relation to boost pressure.

The Crane unit uses a dash mounted control knob that allows you set how much timing the ignition should retard relative to boost pressure. You can set the dial to retard from 1°- 3° for every pound of boost pressure. This lets you dial in the ignition from the comfort of the driver's seat.

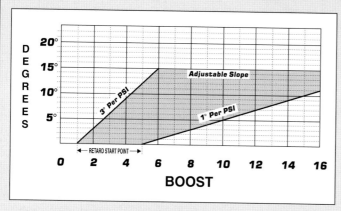

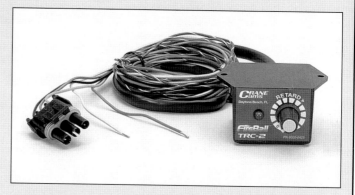

This chart shows the relationship between the engine's boost pressure and the amount of timing retard that you can adjust.

A boost retard timing control lets you select an amount of timing retard that occurs in relation to the boost pressure in the engine. This Crane ignition has a boost control dial that mounts to the dash for changes on the fly.

Bolt-Down to Lock Out

If you have an MSD Pro-Billet Distributor with a mechanical advance, it can easily be locked-out. First, remove the springs, weights, and their spacers. Then remove the lock nut that holds the stop bushing in place. Keep the nut handy, as you'll need it again.

Next, you'll need to either remove the gear or the retaining sleeve from the distributor shaft. Ford distributors have gears that are pressed on, so just remove the sleeve. You only need to pull the distributor shaft up a couple inches. Note the position of the little threaded stud where the stop bushing originally was located. Turn the shaft 180° and put the threaded stud in the hole. Install the lock nut and you're officially locked-out!

MSD's distributors allow you to easily lock out the timing. The process is reversible if you ever decide locked-out timing isn't right for your engine.

need to idle smooth, start in hot conditions, and maintain good driveability with varying loads. Your race car is designed to excel under one condition and one condition only — wide open. In this case, why even deal with the centrifugal advance when total timing is really all we're concerned with.

Locked-out timing refers to only having total timing. There is no vacuum or centrifugal advance to add in. This can be accomplished by locking-out the advance mechanism (hence the term) or moving to what's commonly referred to as a crank trigger distributor. Before there was a performance aftermarket, racers would strip the advance components from a distributor and weld the shaft together to make it a solid part. The benefit is solid, total timing. But as with most tuning stages, there are also cons.

Let's say you have the timing locked at 36°. This means there is a lot more pressure on the starter, flexplate, and battery when you try to start the engine, especially after a hot soak on a thick summer day. Advanced timing is not starter friendly and is even worse on a hot engine. This is because the spark is starting the combustion process earlier in the piston's combustion stroke, and the engine is only at 200-250 rpm during cranking. The only inertia the piston has going for it is from the starter, and the advanced combustion process puts a lot of pressure on the slow-moving piston. This is one of the main reasons that a centrifugal or electronic advance is built into most distributors.

For race cars, this problem can be overcome by with a stout gear reduction starter and strong battery that you keep charged between rounds. Plus, there are other electronic accessories available that will provide a retard while the engine is cranking.

TIME FOR A CRANK TRIGGER?

If you've decided that locked-out timing is right for your application, then you should pony up and consider moving to a crank trigger ignition system. A crank trigger is the most accurate way to trigger the ignition throughout high-RPM operation.

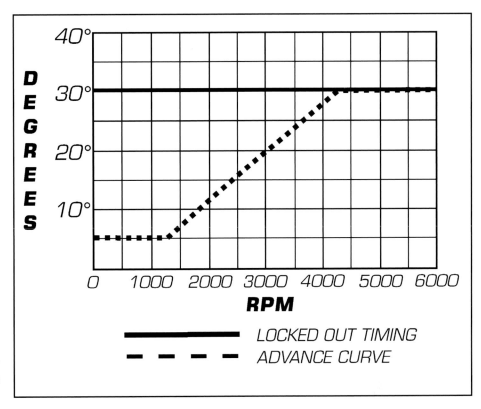

The dotted line illustrates the centrifugal advance curve compared to the locked-out timing shown in the solid line. The locked-out timing is good on race cars, but may not be street friendly due to increased cranking pressures, detonation, and idle speeds.

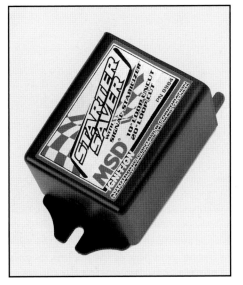

When you have locked-out timing the engine may crank slower or even kick back after a hot soak. Many timing controls are available that will retard the timing when the engine is cranking to make it easier to roll the engine over. This compact unit from MSD retards the timing either 10° or 20° until the engine reaches about 800 rpm.

When it comes to precise trigger signals, you can't beat a crank trigger system. Even most distributorless ignitions receive their trigger signal from the crankshaft.

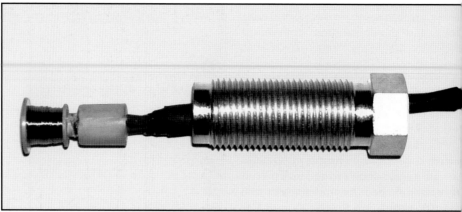

The non-magnetic pickup of a "flying magnet" crank trigger can only be triggered by the magnets in the wheel. This makes false triggering due to track debris or other metal objects impossible. Note the arrow on the wheel denoting rotation of the engine. The wheel must be installed correctly or the timing will be affected.

A non-magnetic pickup is similar to a coil. It has a coil of windings around an iron core that together produce a voltage signal when a magnet passes through its path.

A crank trigger system provides the same service as the pickup inside a distributor to trigger the ignition control. The benefit of the crank trigger is that the trigger signal comes directly from the crankshaft, and what other engine component is more closely related to piston position and engine RPM? By having the trigger come directly from the crankshaft, you bypass mechanical variables from vibration frequencies and flexing that occur through the timing chain and its gears, the cam-gear to distributor-gear, and even the distributor shaft.

Crank trigger kits are available from most performance ignition companies. Most operate by installing an aluminum trigger wheel to the dampener of the crankshaft. This wheel will have four (on V-8 engines, three on 6 cylinders) magnets positioned 90° from each other. These magnets produce a signal that triggers the ignition as they spin past a stationary non-magnetic pickup that is mounted close to the edge of the wheel.

When the aftermarket first developed the crank trigger in the mid 1980s, a magnetic pickup was mounted near the balancer on the engine. The trigger wheel had metal studs that would create

Magnet position is imperative in the wheel. Notice how they are angled in the wheel. As the magnet passes the pickup, its polarity changes and the voltage signal swings to positive, creating the trigger signal.

a trigger signal instead of magnets. The trouble with this design was that the magnetic pickup could be falsely triggered by another bolt or metal object, even from crankshaft flex. By using the same theory but by making the magnets the only thing that can trigger the non-magnetic pickup, you get a system that can't be false triggered.

Setting Up A Crank Trigger

Installing a crank trigger system is pretty straightforward, as most kits come with the brackets and accessories you'll need for a complete installation. One aspect you need to consider is that the trigger wheel bolts to the balancer, which means the belt pulley will be spaced further out. This means you'll

If you need to make small timing adjustments on your crank trigger, look into one of these add-on timing adjusters. These let you adjust the position of the pickup through a threaded stud resulting in precision timing changes.

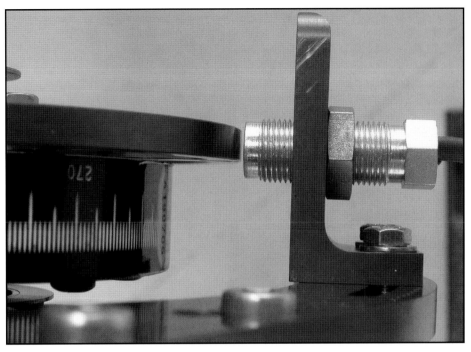

The pickup must be aligned with the centerline of the trigger wheel's edge as shown. Being off could adversely affect the strength of the signal. The air gap should be in the range of 0.035 - 0.060 inch and will not change the performance level of the engine.

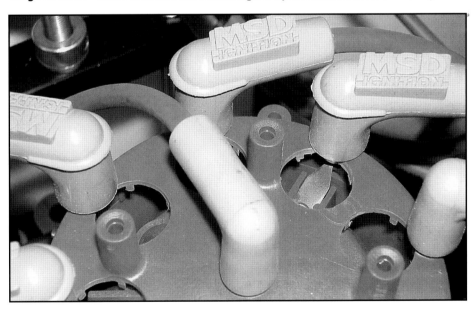

Since the timing is controlled by the crank trigger pickup, you only need to position the distributor so the number-1 cap terminal is aligned with the rotor tip when the engine is sitting at the desired timing.

have to compensate the extra width by moving any belt driven accessories out the same distance.

One of the most important things is ensuring that the trigger wheel is centered on the balancer. Most trigger wheels have a couple different bolt patterns as well as a centering ring for different applications. With the trigger wheel installed, mount the brackets and pickup. Usually there are spacers supplied with the kit, so you can position the pickup on the centerline of the trigger wheel. The next step is to adjust the gap between the pickup and the wheel.

The air gap is not like a spark plug gap, since it doesn't affect performance. Essentially, the pickup needs to be close enough to create a trigger at cranking speeds. If the engine starts, the pickup is close enough. Conversely, on big cubic-inch engines at high RPM, there can be excessive crankshaft flexing, so you don't want the pickup to be too close to where contact gets made. The gap should be .050 – .080 inch.

To set the timing, position the number one cylinder at the desired timing BTDC. Slide the pickup until it is aligned with the closest magnet and tighten it in place. Start the engine and check the timing with a light. If the timing is off or is varying, check the wiring of the pickup, as the polarity of the wires must be correct. If the polarity is swapped, the timing will vary. Once the timing is set, you'll need to move to the distributor to simply line up the number one plug wire terminal with the rotor tip.

CRANK TRIGGER DISTRIBUTORS

Once you have a crank trigger handling the trigger chores, the distributor's responsibility drops to simply distributing the spark. Of course, it is still important to have a solid housing and shaft assembly but another benefit is that you can run a shorter distributor. This is a terrific option when firewall or exotic intake combinations cause space

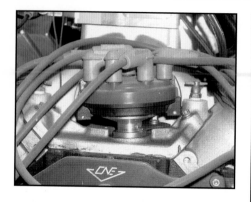

An extra-short distributor can be used when a crank trigger kit is handling the ignition triggering chores. With no pick-up or advance, these distributors are extra low, so there's more room for outlandish intake combinations.

The crab-cap crank trigger distributor is needed on many Pro Stock and Pro Street cars that have limited space for the distributor due to custom intake manifolds and firewall clearance issues. Note the small diameter of the cap compared to the Ford-style cap.

to be at premium. There are several versions of these distributors available and they can be smaller or shorter since they don't have to make room for a pickup or advance assembly. There's simply a rotor connected to the distributor shaft and a cap!

Some distributors are available with a Ford-style cap, which is desirable because of its large diameter. If things are too tight for this cap, Mallory and MSD both offer a distributor with what's commonly referred to as a "crab cap." This cap features terminals that stick out to the side rather than out of the top of the cap. This really opens up the area around the distributor. The down side to this distributor is that the cap is quite small, but in many cases, it is the only answer. It will work just like it is supposed to, but again, going with

Be Positive on Polarity

A non-magnetic pickup has polarity just like a magnetic pickup and must be connected to the ignition control correctly. If the polarity is switched, the timing will be adversely affected, resulting in rough running or even backfiring. How much it affects the timing depends on the ignition control and the pickup being used. Regardless, make sure to get it right.

PICKUP	POLARITY POSITIVE	POLARITY NEGATIVE
Moroso Crank Trigger Pickup	White	Black
MSD Crank Trigger Pickup	Violet	Green
Mallory Crank Trigger Pickup	Violet	Green

These are some common polarity listings. If the polarity is reversed, your timing will be adversely affected.

The crank trigger pickup plugs into the same magnetic pickup connector of your ignition control. Even though one is a magnetic pickup while the other is a non-magnetic pickup, they create the same style voltage signal. The same care should be taken when routing the harness. Make sure it is away from heat sources, but also keep it separate from the spark plug wires or even coil primary wiring. Keeping it routed along a ground plane such as the frame or a chassis bar is a good idea to help prevent interference. For the best protection against electro magnetic interference, use a shielded cable. These offer a grounded sleeve for the pickup wires resulting in the best EMI protection.

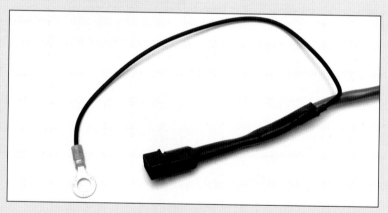

A shielded magnetic pickup harness has a special sleeve that attaches to ground. This creates a barrier against electrical interference from other accessories and high-voltage components on your car.

the larger style cap is always the recommended way to go.

ROTOR PHASING

With a crank trigger handling the ignition trigger chores, the distributor is left the simple task of transferring the high voltage from the coil to the correct distributor terminal at the right moment. All you need to do is simply line up the rotor tip and the distributor cap terminal at your desired timing. This alignment between the rotor tip

Front Drive

What if there is just no possible way that you can get a distributor in your engine? Racers always find a way. If room is a premium you could go with a front-mount distributor.

A front-drive distributor mounts vertically to the front of the motor and is driven from a pulley and belt that is installed to the timing gear. Obviously, a belt driven cam is required, so this system is mainly for high-performance racing engines. Jesel and Comp Cams have belt drive camshaft kits and Jesel offers a front-drive distributor to complete their kit. Moving to a front-mount distributor makes routing the plug wires easy, there's less heat to deal with and the belt drive absorbs mechanical harmonics from the cam and crank.

A front-drive distributor is a popular solution for tight engine compartments and intake setups. By using a belt drive on the camshaft, a front-drive distributor can be incorporated by running a belt off the camshaft to turn the distributor. Jesel, Mallory, and MSD all have front-mount distributor kits.

The major gain is space in the rear of the engine of course! Plus, swapping intakes becomes easier without having to bother with a distributor and rotor phasing. Plus, inspection of the cap and rotor are easier.

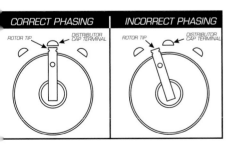

This diagram illustrates correct rotor phasing and what happens when it is off. On distributors with small caps, you can see how easily the spark could jump to the next terminal resulting in crossfire and possible pre-ignition.

which could result in a miss or crossfire to another cylinder.

On a single-stage nitrous system that only requires a few degrees of retard when the system is active, the rotor phasing will be slightly off, but as long as everything in the secondary side of the ignition is in good condition, it should not pose a problem. Remember that the degrees of change in the distributor are half that of the crankshaft. Depending on the size and condition of the cap and rotor, it is when you get up over 8° of retard that you really need to be concerned with adjusting the rotor phasing.

As the nitrous dose or even boost pressure get larger, more timing needs to be pulled out. For instance, if a racer is pulling out 14° of timing when the nitrous is activated, the rotor tip is well past the cap terminal when the ignition fires. So you already are putting higher pressures against the ignition system with the phasing off not to mention the increased cylinder pressures from the nitrous being injected into the mix. This all adds up to higher voltage being required to jump the gap along with more reasons for a misfire. If you're at this level of performance, the rotor phasing must be checked and set!

On race cars, it is important that the rotor phasing be aligned when the engine is racing and all of the retard rates are active. It is easier for the phasing to be off a couple degrees when the engine is idling and cylinder pressures are low than when the engine is under increased cylinder pressures or at high RPM.

How much timing you are pulling out affects where to set the rotor phasing. A high-horsepower nitrous engine may require as much as 20° of retard! In extreme cases like this, it may be best to split the difference in the phasing. For example, if you are pulling out 15° of timing, set the phasing at about 10° (crankshaft degrees). This will throw the phasing off 10° at idle and low speeds, and at high RPM, it will only be off by 5°, which should not present any troubles.

Checking and Setting Rotor Phasing

To check the rotor phasing, locate an old distributor cap that you can

and the cap terminal is called rotor phasing. It sounds simple enough, but what happens when you start to manipulate the timing?

On engines that are using electronic retard controls such as the ones used with nitrous, the rotor phasing becomes extremely important. When the timing is retarded, the spark occurs after the rotor tip passes the cap terminal. This means it takes more voltage to jump across the gap, which puts more pressure on the secondary side of the ignition. Worse yet, the spark may start looking for an easier path to ground,

The best way to check phasing is to drill a large hole in the cap right at one of the terminals. Then, with the engine running put your timing light on that cylinder and watch the spark as it jumps the gap.

modify. Choose a terminal of the cap that will be easy to view while the cap is installed and the engine is running. Drill a hole that is large enough so you can see the plug wire terminal post and the rotor tip. With the cap installed, connect your timing light to the spark plug wire that runs to the terminal you can see. With the engine running, you'll be able to see the position of the rotor tip as the spark jumps across to the wire, and you'll be able to align it correctly. Remember to activate any retard controls to view where the phasing is during a run down the track.

Crank trigger ignition systems and rotor phasing are mostly found on race engines. These are important parts and procedures in getting the spark to the plug at the exact moment. With a crank trigger generally comes electronic timing controls that we touched on at the start of this chapter. There are numerous controls available that produce a preprogrammed timing curve, versions that provide stages of retard, models that let you program an entire curve, and just about anything else you can think of for your timing. Chapter 9 will introduce more of these timing controls and functions that give you so much more control over your timing.

Can You Phase It?

Can rotor phasing be adjusted if you're using the pickup inside a locked-out distributor? This gets difficult, since the pickup inside the distributor is generally mounted in one place and is not adjustable. About the only choice is to reposition the pickup, which would take some time and a lot of machine work. An alternative is the adjustable rotor Cap-A-Dapt kit from MSD.

This kit fits many of MSD's distributors and most models that accept a GM points style cap. There are two pieces to the rotor, a base, and a top with slotted holes. This allows the phasing to be adjusted by rotating the top piece. Also, you get the benefit of a larger diameter cap for improved spark isolation.

MSD's Cap-A-Dapt with two-piece rotor provides an easy way to set the rotor phasing. Also, the larger diameter cap lessens the chance of spark scatter from occurring within the cap.

Rotor Tips and Conditions

Another important feature of rotor phasing is the condition of the rotor itself. Worn and burned tips and terminals are not going to make it any easier on getting the lazy voltage to go to the right place at the right moment. Voltage likes to build up on a sharp edge to jump a gap, so having a rotor tip in prime condition is important. In most cases, simply treating the cap and rotor as a maintenance item throughout the race season will suffice.

MSD found that on their higher-output ignitions and magnetos that a special rotor tip helped in the life and performance of the secondary side of the ignition. The rotor tip has one rounded corner and one edge at a right angle. There is also an arrow denoting the rotation of the distributor. By positioning the rotor tip so the sharp corner is the trailing edge of the rotor's rotation, there will be less chance of spark scatter. This tip is only available on their extra large Pro-Cap.

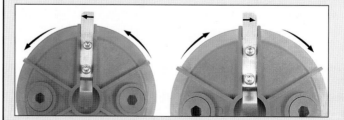

This special rotor tip was designed to improve the control of the voltage delivery on high-output race-only ignitions such as the Pro Mag 44. The tip is reversible depending on your engine's rotation. It is also helpful when using timing retards.

RPM AND TIMING CONTORLS

Now that you have your timing locked out and understand the importance of rotor phasing, we'll delve into the world of electronic timing controls. There are a variety of controls offered that you can easily wire into to your current ignition system to gain more adjustment. The aftermarket ignition companies are taking their most popular timing accessories and are building them right into their new ignition controls. But you can't please everyone all the time, so some systems won't have the options you need. Or what if you already have a lot invested in your ignition system and just need a single stage of retard? Going with an add-on timing control is the answer for many enthusiasts.

An electronic timing control replaces the centrifugal advance mechanism taking those troublesome mechanical inefficiencies out of the picture. Both serve the same purpose, to match the timing with the engine's load and RPM, but the electronic systems can

Timing controls give you an entirely new area to tune for performance. Top Fuel cars take advantage of up to three MSD Six Shooter Retard Controls to alter the timing up to 16 times within a 4-second pass! This illustrates the use of step retards to the extreme, since most performance applications will be set with one, two, or three stages.

Some racers actually advance the timing at certain points during a pass to gain torque. In order to advance the timing electronically, you need to advance the total timing by moving the trigger device or distributor, and then compensate for it by setting the timing control.

The Start Retard Control from MSD provides a single retard step that is adjustable with plug-in modules, similar to RPM chips. This unit also has a retard feature that is activated during cranking to ease the pressure placed on the starter. Once the engine starts, the timing will return to the mechanical set timing.

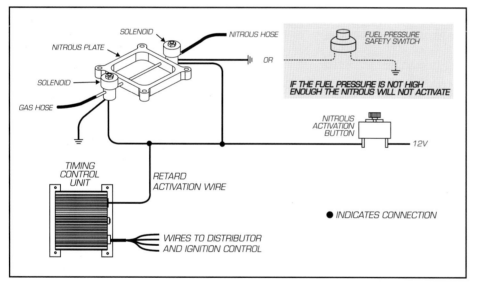

Here is an example of wiring a single step retard with a nitrous plate system. The retard will be activated when the nitrous button is pressed.

deliver much more control. Other benefits are that they are more accurate, they can react faster, they are repeatable, and they allow you to set a variety of functions.

Electronic timing controls always wire between the trigger device and the ignition control. By getting the signal first, it can pause or retard the signal by

the amount you select, and then send it to the ignition to fire the coil. It was mentioned, but it is worth bringing up again, that there is no way a timing control can advance the ignition timing! A timing control can only retard the timing from the total timing that you set with the crank trigger or distributor. In order to advance the timing, you need

set the total timing more advanced than normal and make up for that difference through the timing control.

Electronic timing controls open a large window of tuning possibilities. With the advances in technology and information racers gather from data acquisition systems, the advanced timing controls that are coming out provide endless tuning possibilities. Before getting into these cutting-edge systems, we'll start with one of the most popular types of electronic timing controls, the step retard device.

STEP RETARDS

A step retard control will activate a step or stage of retard at a selected moment. Generally there is an activation wire that enables the retard step when you need it. An example is when a nitrous solenoid is turned on. This is the most common application, since the introduction of nitrous and oxygen into the combustion chamber causes the engine to require less timing advance. Being able to enable a timing retard only when the nitrous system is active provides the best use of your ignition timing.

To control the activation of the retard step, the control will have a corresponding wire that needs to be con-

Nitrous HP = Degrees of Retard

Nitrous oxide is made up of two nitrogen molecules, with one oxygen molecule stuck in the mix. That molecule of oxygen does wonders for performance when it is mixed properly with the correct amount of fuel. Remember, it's not the nitrous that makes the power; it's the extra fuel you can burn thanks to the oxygen. Also, the intake charge is cooled because the nitrous absorbs heat as it changes from a liquid state to a gas. This increases the density and oxygen content. The burn rate of the air/fuel mixture is increased, which means the timing must be retarded to compensate.

How much retard you need is dependent on how much nitrous oxide is being introduced. A rule of thumb is 2° of retard for every 50 horsepower shot of nitrous. It is best to retard the timing too much than to not retard enough! After an initial pass, pull all of the plugs — yes ALL of the plugs — to get an idea if you're too rich or a little lean. Cylinders can have slight variances in the way they perform, so it is important to check each spark plug.

The Multi-Stage Retard from Mallory has three stages that are adjustable with rotary dials. Each retard step overrides the other steps, so you could pull 8° out the first step, then only 4° for step two, and back up 12° for stage three.

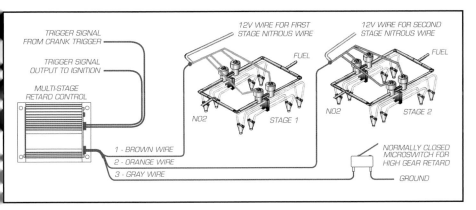

This diagram illustrates a typical multi-step retard control wiring with a two-stage nitrous system. The control receives the trigger signal first, and then it goes to the ignition box. The retard activation wires are spliced into the nitrous solenoids' 12-volt wires. So when the nitrous button is pushed, the retard is activated. After the pass, when the nitrous is turned off, the timing returns to the set amount.

nected to 12 volts (in most cases) or removed from ground to retard the timing. (Be sure to check with the control's manufacturer on how to wire their system.) An example is to splice the activation wire into the nitrous solenoid's switching 12-volt supply wire. This way, the timing will be retarded as soon as the nitrous is activated.

Multi-Step Retards

Just as the name implies, multi-step retard controls do just that — provide several stages of retard. These of course are designed specifically for multi-stage nitrous systems. Generally, there are three or four separate retard steps, and each step has its own activation wire. Depending on the system you use, these steps can either be cumulative when activated together, or each stage can cancel the other when activated. Both systems have their place and use.

As an example, with a cumulative multi-stage nitrous system you may take 8° of timing out with the first stage, 6° more with the second, and an additional 2° with the third stage. This brings a total retard of 16° at top end (8 + 6 + 2 = 16). Being able to program a different amount for each stage provides a lot of control over each stage. If the tuneup changes and more nitrous is used during the third stage instead of the second, the amounts of retard can easily be switched around.

A sequential retard control keeps each retard rate independent as they override each other. When the second stage is activated, whatever amount of retard that step one was pulling out is deactivated and the second stage retard rate is enabled. A third stage would override both step one and two. This system is can be beneficial if you decide to put timing back in at a certain points. For instance, if you really want to kill some power coming off the line, you may retard the timing 15° then for the second stage it could be programmed for only 8° since the car is rolling and the tires are already hooking up.

Most timing retards will limit the amount of retard that you can use to 25° – 30°. The biggest reason for this limit is the rotor phasing and distributor cap. Twenty-five degrees of retard is about the maximum that a standard size distributor cap and rotor can handle. You don't want to get into spark scatter when you have a huge hit of nitrous being poured into your engine.

Of course, there are many other different applications for a step retard than just with nitrous. Many engine builders like to pull a couple degrees of timing out at top end or high RPM, which can be accomplished with a micro-switch on the shifter. Some racers

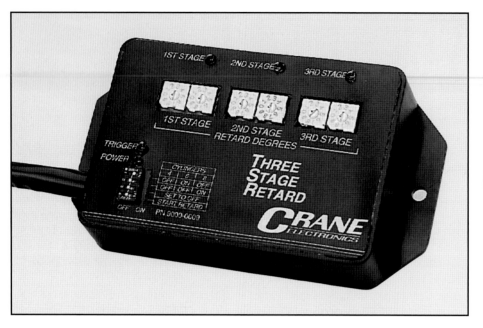

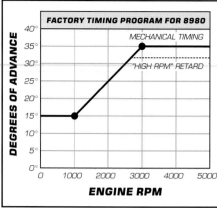

This is the timing curve that is preprogrammed into MSD's PN 8980 Timing Control. This is an average timing curve and will work well in street cars and race applications. There is also a single-step retard option built in.

The Crane Three Stage Retard offers three adjustable retards that are cumulative up to 30°. Each stage is adjusted with rotary dials plus there is an automatic start retard feature. Note that there are switches to select a 4, 6, or 8-cylinder engine. Most timing controls can be used on different engine configurations.

Retard to Get Rollin'

There are a lot of 'street legal' drag classes that impose limits on the size of the slicks or even mandate a drag radial. These cars may be stretching the street-legal term like a big block in a Yugo, but the point is that they make huge amounts of power! Much more than a 10.5-inch tire can handle, so racers are challenged with getting the car to launch instead of looking like contestants in a burnout contest. What does this have to do with timing controls you ask? Everything.

Many small-tire cars will set up a timer to activate or deactivate a stage of retard on the holeshot. By wiring the retard to be activated as soon as the car launches, the power of the engine can be compromised just enough to the get tires planted. Once the tires are hooked and rolling, the timer deactivates the retard as the tires are able to accept more power once the car is launched and moving down the track.

By incorporating a timer such as a Digi-Set from NOS, a retard step can be activated during the launch of the car. As soon as the transbrake is released, the timer turns on, activating the first stage of retard. Once timed out, the retard step is deactivated and the timing returns to the set amount.

are doing just the opposite by putting timing back into the engine at higher RPM in an effort to boost the engine's torque curve. This could be handled with an RPM activated switch set up to turn a retard off at a desired RPM.

Most of these examples have been in drag racing applications, so what about on a circle track car? You could wire each stage to a toggle switch on the dash so the driver could pull timing out as track conditions go south. This of course would have to be legal to do in your racing sanction, but it does illustrate the different uses. Multi-step retards could provide one stage as a helpful stating retard, while the other stages would be used for normal retard functions. Perhaps a step could be wired into an RPM switch so the timing would be retarded at a high RPM to soften some power output. Use your imagination and review your rulebook.

TIMING CURVE CONTROLS

Perhaps you would prefer a timing curve similar to that of a centrifugal advance, instead of retards that are either on or off. The benefit of going electronic is an accurate, consistent ignition curve. In many cases you can program the curve by turning a dial or flipping a switch rather than changing advance springs, weights, or stop bushings.

If you find that you simply need an ignition curve to help your locked-out car in the cranking and idling department, the MSD preprogrammed timing control is a good choice. At an idle, this control will retard the timing 20° from your total timing. This is especially helpful during cranking. At 1,000 rpm, the timing will begin to advance and by 3,000 rpm the timing will be back at the total amount. This is about as basic as an electronic advance comes.

If you would like to have a little more control over the timing curve, here are more options. The MSD Programmable Timing Control allows you to program how much the timing is retarded from the total setting, the RPM point that the advance begins, and the rate at which the timing is brought back in. These adjustments are made through three potentiometers on the side of the unit's housing. When setting up a timing curve on a control like this, a timing light and tachometer are essential. After those, the best tool you can have is time and a place to test and tune.

INDIVIDUAL CYLINDER TIMING

In recent years, one of the best timing control features that has been developed is the ability to adjust the timing in each cylinder. No two combustion chambers are absolutely alike or require the exact same amount of timing. This is due to a variety of issues ranging from the intake manifold design, to the material of the heads, the location of the valves, and so on. These slight differences are even highlighted more in nitrous applications, due to the increased cylinder pressures and the introduction of more oxygen and fuel into the chamber.

Circle track racers have been modifying the distributor's reluctor for years in order to modify the timing of different cylinders. NASCAR rules mandate a distributor triggered ignition and no electronic timing controls can be used. This forces them to dig into the distributor to make their own modifications. This is no easy task and it also limits the use of each modified distributor to certain engines only. For those of us stuck

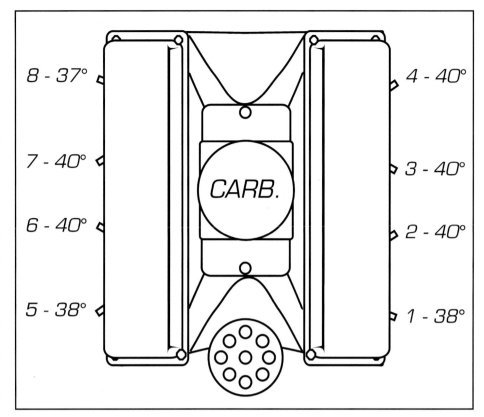

This diagram illustrates where a couple different cylinders could use less timing. Generally these cylinders are inhibited due to flow restrictions or varying temperatures. Knowing your engine and reading plugs are the most popular way to set the cylinder timing, but reading separate EGTs is the most effective.

in the real performance world, cylinder-to-cylinder timing can now be accomplished easily through electronic timing controls.

What's the benefit of cylinder-to-cylinder timing? Consider the oft-used adage, 'One bad apple spoils the whole bunch.' When you set the timing of your engine at 34°, you are setting it at 34° for every cylinder. But that may not be ideal in every hole. If you have one or two cylinders that run leaner than the other cylinders, you have to compromise for these bad apples. This results in the other cylinders running a touch off their ideal timing setting and a compromise in your engine's output. Compromising power is not something that engine builders and racers ever want to hear about.

Individual cylinder timing is certainly not for every performance car out there, but for racers running on the top-end, it is extremely important. Several years ago many drag racers moved to

EFI systems due to the advanced control it gave them in tuning. In talking with a couple racers at street events, we were told that some never would have converted to EFI had they had the ability to control cylinder timing through the ignition system. This is another place that racers can find just that little bit more to give them a push over the competition. Or in a nitrous application, being able to pull back a couple cylinders can help keep all of the cylinders happy. (By happy we mean not going lean and burning pistons.) Like we mentioned, circle track cars have been messing with cylinder timing for years by modifying the distributor's reluctor, but until recently, cars with crank triggers couldn't do a lot to compensate for a couple less-than-perfect flowing cylinders.

In order to program timing for individual cylinders, the controller or ignition must be able to identify which cylinder is number one. This is needed so

Mechanical Individual Cylinder Timing

Many racing sanctioning bodies do not allow the use of electronic timing devices, and whether they like it or not, racers need to abide by these rules. This promotes a serious amount of reading between the lines in certain cases, but it can also lead to new product ideas.

Engine builders can go into the distributor to bend or machine the reluctor or paddle in order to alter a cylinder's timing. By slightly repositioning one of the paddles in the direction of its rotation, the timing of that cylinder will be advanced. By going against the rotation, it will retard the timing. The trouble is that these paddles were never intended to be repositioned, so they're easy to break! Moroso, MSD, and Precision Machine offer a billet steel reluctor that accepts machining and modifying much better than the powdered metal counterparts that are used in most distributors.

There are also a couple advanced racing distributors offered for these applications. The end of Chapter 9 gets into more information about setting these high-end distributors up for individual cylinder timing.

The individual cylinder timing system on MSD's Multi-Function Controller incorporates an easy to install fiber-inductive pickup. This slips over the number-1 spark plug wire so the pickup can reference the number-1 cylinder. A fiber optic cable connects to the controller so EMI cannot interfere.

A billet-steel reluctor can be machined to alter each cylinder's timing. This is important in high-end race engines such as those used in stock car racing where electronic controls are not legal. Optically triggered distributors can also be modified by machining the openings of their trigger discs.

it knows when your unique retard order begins. Some controls allow you to program a firing order, while on others you may need to list your cylinders in a consecutive order. In this case you need to pay close attention when you're setting the cylinders. You don't want to retard the wrong cylinder! The DC9500 Digital Engine Control from Crane needs a cam sync signal, which can be accomplished by installing a non-magnetic pickup kit to the cam gear or by using a distributor with a cam sync pickup built in. As long as you're using a crank trigger, you can remove all but one of the paddles from a distributor that uses a magnetic pickup and use its signal. If this is done, you'll need to pay attention to its phasing as well as the rotor phasing.

Once there is a cam sync and the engine is running, where do you start?

Hopefully you already have a good idea of how your engine runs and an idea on what cylinders you would like to retard from reading the spark plugs. One idea for cylinder timing is to run the engine on a dyno or in the car with exhaust gas temperature (EGT) probes in each header tube just outside the cylinder. With testing time, you can quickly identify the best timing per cylinder when the optimum cylinder temperature is achieved. If this procedure is not within your plans, reading the spark plugs and paying attention to your engine and tune up will point you in the right direction.

Add-on accessory controls with cylinder-to-cylinder timing capabilities are available from Crane and MSD. Crane allows you to retard each cylinder up to 10°, which in most cases is

This Hand Held Dyno Tuning Control from MSD allows you to change the timing of each cylinder instantly so you can make quick changes and watch their effect on the exhaust gas temperature. You can play with this until the optimum timing setting is recorded in each cylinder.

plenty. It doesn't take a lot of timing retard to alter the ability of each cylinder. These are nice because you do not have to replace your entire ignition system. On the downside, you do need to mount another box on your car, and have other wiring to contend with. Most of these controllers will do much more than just ICT including detailed timing curves and RPM controls. We will get into these advanced controllers after discussing RPM controls and their benefits.

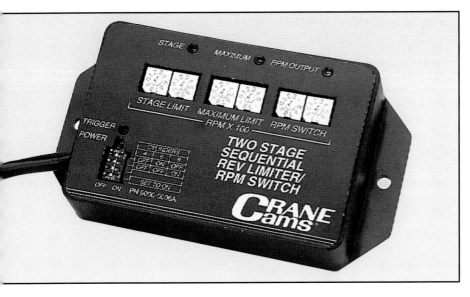

Crane offers a two- or three- stage rev limiter that can be added to most aftermarket capacitive discharge ignition controls. This model lets you decide between a third RPM limit and an RPM-activated switch.

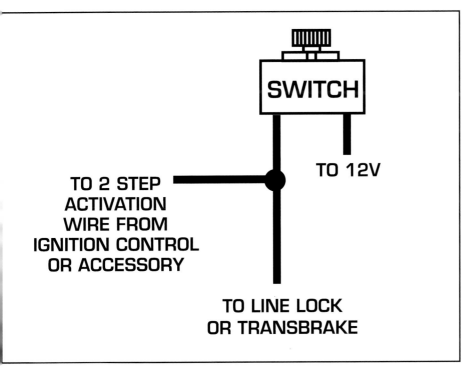

This diagram shows how easy it is to add an MSD Two Step Module Selector to your existing ignition control. Depending on your transmission, you can either connect the low limit to be active with a transbrake or linelock.

USING RPM TO YOUR ADVANTAGE

Engine RPM also presents you with a good area to tune in performance. Generally, you wouldn't think of an RPM limiter as a function to improve performance, but by using it off the line can help improve reaction times while providing consistent launches. Also, you can use RPM points to activate a circuit such as a shift point or even turn on a nitrous solenoid. It all adds up to improved control through consistency and tuning.

RPM Limiters

The two main features that you have control over in the ignition system are timing and RPM. Rev limiters may not be a factor in finding more power numbers from the engine, but knowing how your car and engine react to different RPM levels is important. Holeshot RPM and shift points help produce consistency, while an over-rev RPM limit can save your engine.

RPM limiters were devised to help save engines from over-rev damage, but this technology was quickly employed for other tasks. Sure, most race cars on a road course or drag strip still have a rev limiter for high-RPM protection, but when it comes to tuning, the rev limiter is an important tool on the starting line.

Drag racers were quick to realize the benefits of being able to activate a different rev limit during the holeshot. This feature is most commonly referred to as a two-step rev limiter. The two-step gives you two rev limits that can be programmed for different uses. By activating a rev limit on the starting line, you can improve your consistency for bracket racing tuning the suspension and car around a common holeshot RPM. A rev limiter can also improve your reaction time, since you don't need to concentrate on the launch RPM.

The two-step is a simple switching device. There is an activation wire for one of the limits that is activated generally by supplying 12 volts. This is usually accomplished by splicing this wire into the 12-volt feed line that connects to the trans brake or line-lock solenoid. When the Christmas tree goes green and the switch is released, the voltage is gone and the two-step switches to the high side RPM limit for over-rev protection.

The common drag racer way of thinking is that if one is good, two is better, so three has to be the even better yet! Thus, the three-step rev limiter is born. The idea in most cases here is to be able to set a rev limit for use during the burnout. Not only does this keep the RPM lower than the high-side limit, but it can also aid in keeping tire temperatures within a consistent range.

Most of the new drag racing ignitions have a two-step built in, or there

In the Clutch with a Holeshot Limit

So you still like to stir the gearbox in your drag car (good for you), but want to activate the two-step off the clutch switch. This can easily be accomplished with a micro-switch mounted off the clutch pedal. But wait a second — won't the two-step be activated every time you push the clutch in? Yes, indeed it will, unless you get a little creative in your wiring with a relay. By wiring in a relay, you can activate the two-step rev limit through the clutch switch and latch on to line lock at the same time. This means the clutch switch will control the launch RPM and line lock at the same time.

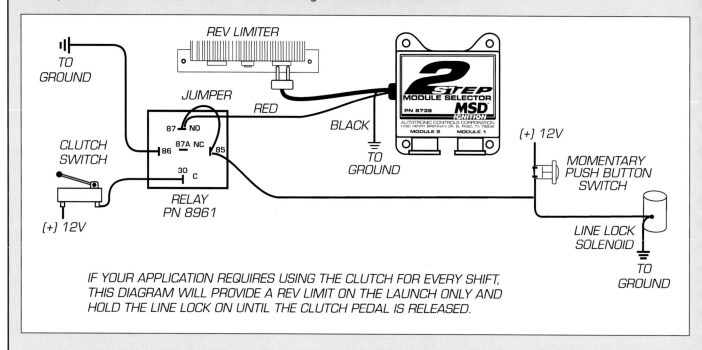

IF YOUR APPLICATION REQUIRES USING THE CLUTCH FOR EVERY SHIFT, THIS DIAGRAM WILL PROVIDE A REV LIMIT ON THE LAUNCH ONLY AND HOLD THE LINE LOCK ON UNTIL THE CLUTCH PEDAL IS RELEASED.

By using a relay, you can activate the holeshot rev limit through the clutch pedal and line-lock solenoid. This way the rev limit will only be active on the starting line, not while you shift gears as you race down the track.

are accessories that will give you the ability to add a two-step to your current ignition. In most cases, to add a two-step your current CD ignition, it must already have a rev limiter built in. You cannot add an MSD Two-step Module Selector to a 6A, because it does not have the rev limiting circuitry in the ignition. Since a 6AL or 7AL-2 already have the MSD Soft Touch rev controlling circuits, a two-step selector can be added.

RPM Switches

If you want to activate a component at a certain engine RPM, you'll need an RPM-activated switch. These devices are extremely helpful when turning on a nitrous solenoid, activating an air shifter, or even for something as simple as turning on a shift light.

There are several versions of these switches available, but they all work in a similar fashion. They all connect to the tach signal of the ignition control and provide a ground path to complete a circuit at the certain RPM that you set. There are some models that give you the option of supplying a ground path, or opening the ground path. One thing to watch for though is when you want to activate a high-current component such as a nitrous solenoid, you'll need to wire in a relay. Most RPM switches can't handle more than an amp of draw. Generally, a switch can be used on 4, 6, or 8-cylinder engines, either with inductive ignitions or CD controls. For distributorless ignitions with waste-spark systems, watch out because the RPM signals will be different. Check with the manufacturer and their specs to make sure the switch you choose will fit your application.

This is just a sampling of the available RPM controls that are available and what can be accomplished with them. As both the manufacturers and the racers embrace computer technology, even more RPM controls have and will become available. Also, there seems to be more add-on accessories that combine RPM functions with adjustable timing features so racers can get a little of both sides of ignition tuning in one unit.

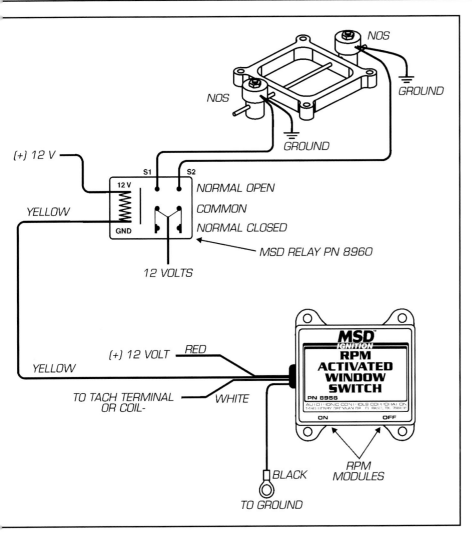

This diagram shows an MSD RPM-Activated Window switch wired to turn on a nitrous solenoid at 3,600 rpm. The "window" portion means it will deactivate the same circuit at a higher RPM. In this case, it is set for 6,800 rpm, so it will turn off the juice before the rev limiter kicks in (set at 7,000 rpm).

CONTROLLERS THAT DO IT ALL

Technology in racing moves as fast as the cars, and there are constantly new controls and ways to make adjustments being introduced. It's not uncommon to see racers sitting in their cars with laptops plugged in to review acquired data or make changes to the ECU. Some of the sanctioning bodies may not like the idea of too much ignition control, but the racers sure seem to like it.

Another benefit to digital technology is being able to combine the most popular timing and RPM accessories into one convenient package. Now you can have a three-step rev limiter, multi-stage retard, a start retard, and an RPM-activated switch all in one control — and have better control and adjustment through all of them! These all encompassing controllers are managed by a microprocessor and can be programmed with a PC or laptop.

Remember the window of tuning opportunity that we discussed earlier? Well, these multi-task controllers and ignitions with all the latest bells and whistles open it even more with unique features that were never possible before. Being able to dial in an electronic timing curve and have rev limits are still important aspects, but now you can actually program a curve down to .1°!

The DEC9500 Digital Engine Control from Crane is digitally controlled add-on accessory that delivers RPM limits, retards, timer functions, an advance curve, and individual cylinder timing. It even allows you to log ignition data to a PC for review. Unlike other controls where you can set the beginning and ending RPM of an ignition curve, this Crane unit lets you program an entire timing curve every 200 rpm in 0.1° increments.

The Crane Control also offers individual cylinder timing that you can program an offset of +/-5° to compen-

The Crane Multi-Function Digital Engine Control wires to CD ignition controls and gives you two rev limits, a start retard, and two-step retards in one convenient and compact component. Settings are determined with rotary dials and a few dip switches.

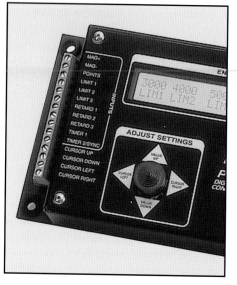

The large LCD screen on the Crane DEC9500 displays all of the adjustable features of the ignition. There is an easy-to-use cursor-type joystick that makes setting a curve or rev limits easy.

You can program MSD's Multi-Function Controller with a handheld monitor or with their Pro-Data+ software from your computer. Both work well but when it comes to plotting an entire RPM curve, the PC makes it much easier, with less chance of error as well.

sate for troublesome cylinders. Or how about a timer that allows you to set the activation point of a component based on time rather than on RPM (though RPM activation is also there for your programming needs). This unit gives you plenty of ignition tuning capabilities all in one unit and can be used with other companies' ignition controls.

The MSD Multi-Function Controller connects to an MSD CD ignition control and provides you a list of common programming needs and a few different adjustments to boot. Programming its features can be done with a hand-held monitor that they offer separately or through a software program for your PC that comes with the control. MSD's software, Pro-Data+, is Windows based and can even be connected with the engine running while showing in real time the timing changes and RPM of your engine.

The software gives you a timing chart to program an entire timing curve. You can plot the amount of retard and at what RPM you want it to occur with a click of your mouse. Now you can create a timing curve that can be advanced, then retarded, advanced again, pulled back again, and on and on throughout the RPM range of the engine. Two other areas of interest in advanced timing control are: getting tires to hook, and helping engines under boost.

MSD offers another Multi-Function Controller that also incorporates a boost related ignition curve. Rather than setting a curve based on RPM and degrees, the timing is retarded in relation to the boost pressure in the manifold. This is a necessity on forced induction engines, and it's easy to plot on a separate chart with the software supplied with the control.

These are all add-on accessories so you don't have to spend big bucks to benefit from some of these adjustable timing features. If you're shopping for a new ignition system all together, or can sell off your basic ignition control to a buddy, you should be very interested to read on about ignition controls that are packed with power and feature all of these programs and more!

Holeshot Timing Curve

We touched upon taking timing out of the engine during the holeshot to help control tire spin by incorporating a timer and step of retard. MSD's Multi-Function Controller has this feature built-in and takes it to another level.

This controller has a holeshot retard program that lets you select a retard amount that is activated as soon as the car launches. This is done through a control wire spliced into the trans-brake or clutch switch. Once you determine how much timing you wish to retard, you can also set the amount of time that the timing takes to ramp back up to the total timing setting. This can range from 0.1 second to 2.5 seconds. Once that timer runs out, the timing returns to run curve that you've programmed on a different chart.

This is an example of a retard curve used during the launch. The timing retard begins to ramp back to the set timing as soon as the car launches. You adjust the amount of retard and the amount of time it takes to ramp back, in order to soften the hit to the tires.

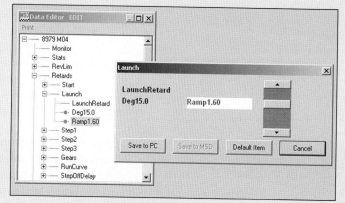

ADVANCED PROGRAMMING

Programming Through Your Computer

Serious racers and engine builders have spent thousands of hours experimenting with timing and RPM functions, searching for any little improvement in power. Until recently though, they were limited to just what they could closely control. The new series of digitally controlled ignition systems and controllers are opening a new window of tuning opportunities for racers to program different aspects of the ignition for their specific application.

Many of the ignitions and controllers we just went over have a lot of adjustable features built into them. Mallory's HyFire VII-S ignition units provide a list of settings and adjustments that are handled through the use of an internal microprocessor. Not only are the ignition controls delivering these great features, but there are also many add-on controllers such as Crane's DEC9500 Digital Engine Control. The Electromotive HPX also offers accurate and easy to program options for timing control and RPM.

After strolling through the pits at a couple drag races ranging from NHRA to the NMCA, we saw a lot of laptops in the cars. Not only were racers and crews downloading info from their data acquisition controls or mapping their EFI controls, but they were also setting up their ignition system. Like it or not, the personal computer is part of motorsports.

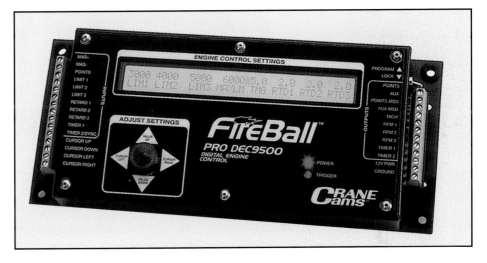

The Crane LCD screen is backlit and easy to read. You scroll through its multitude of programs with a cursor that makes adjustments a breeze. The DEC has the capability to record data from a run and you can even see every firing event through a pass by printing the information or downloading it to a PC with an optional kit.

Actually, once you start to use your these adjustable controllers or through your laptop and see how much you can program and adjust, you'll like it a lot. All of a sudden you'll realize that you can program things you didn't think were possible! Some of these controllers are capable of programming cylinder-to-cylinder timing, mapping an entire advance curve, or maybe one exclusive timing curve for the launch! The list goes on and will probably continue to grow as more PC programmable ignitions are brought into the market.

MSD DIGITAL-7 PROGRAMMABLE

The most popular PC programmable ignition control that we've come across is the MSD Programmable Digital-7 Ignition, PN 7530. MSD has a strong name in ignition performance and this system has certainly made a name for itself. The unit has turned up on classes ranging from Radial Tires to Pro Stock. We felt that taking closer look at this ignition control and its capabilities would be helpful to show you just how much more there is to tune in

---

Between rounds, this racer gets into his laptop to make adjustments to the ignition's timing program or tweak an RPM curve just where he feels it is needed. Tuning with laptops is an important part of performance today.

When you open the Pro-Data+ software, here's what you'll see. There are two timing charts, one for the run, and the other for the launch. On the left there's a program tree, a tach, a retard gauge, a program ladder, and even a place for notes about the run.

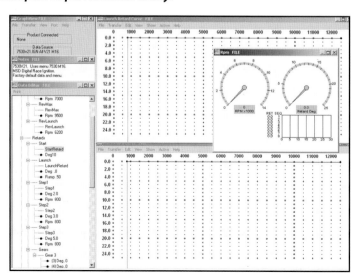

your ignition. The Programmable Digital-7 was their original model and the most popular one in use. They also released a Programmable 7-Plus, PN 7531, ignition with several more features, including a few that got it banned from competition use in NHRA and IHRA racing. We'll touch on a few of its advanced features. First though, we'll get familiar with the operation and programming steps of the original version.

Programming this ignition can be achieved two different ways. For racers that don't have a PC, MSD offers a hand held monitor that has an LCD that you view and skip through a menu of programming options. It works well, but connecting your PC is the way to go. MSD developed their own Windows-based software, the Pro-Data+, which you can download for free on their website. For as many things that you can adjust, the software is surprisingly easy to work with and it won't be long before you feel as comfortable making last minute changes to the timing curve as you do searching Ebay for car parts.

There are several features that you would expect to find in the programs of the Pro-Data+ software. These include things like over-rev, holeshot, and burnout rev limiters, step retards for use with multi-stage nitrous systems, and even a start retard control that will activate automatically when the engine is cranking. This retard shuts off once the engine reaches over 800 rpm. These are features that we've gone over in previous chapters, so we're not going to go over them again. Let's move on to the goodies.

Holeshot Help

The PN 7530 ignition offers several programs to help try to control tire spin to improve your 60-foot times, which is very beneficial for small-tire cars. Many cars are already using retards and timers while this control has them all built-in. First, you'll notice the timing chart on the top right of the screen. This chart is designed for use only during the launch, so you can map a timing curve to fit those needs. When the ignition senses an RPM drop (which you can also pro-

The program tree on the left is where you program the ignition's features. By clicking on the value, another window opens and you simply select the value you want for your program. Here we are adjusting the launch rev limit.

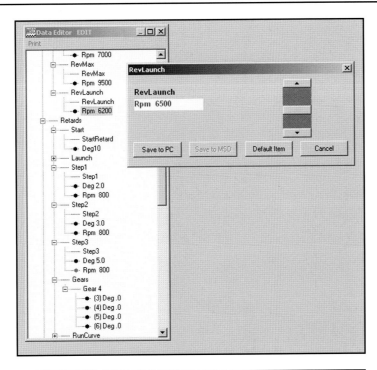

gram) from the shift to second, it switches over to the run curve map that you program in the lower graph.

There is also a time-based retard that is programmed in the menu tree. With this one, you can select an amount of retard that will be activated as soon as the car launches. You also program how long it takes for the timing to ramp back to the total amount. This timed-based retard only happens at the launch.

The Programmable Plus version offers another chart that can be programmed for use during the holeshot, except this one is a ramping RPM limit based on time. You can set an RPM limit during the holeshot that actively changes by ramping to full power in a programmable amount of time. This is much like retarding the timing during a holeshot, except you're using a rev limiter to control the engine's output. This is a new way to consider controlling tire spin off the line. If you like the sounds of this but don't want to upgrade your entire ignition, MSD offers this feature in an add-on controller called the Programmable Launch Controller that can be connected to a 6AL or 7AL-2.

This is an example of a launch curve. If a car leaves the line at 3,000 rpm, it will have full timing until 3,200 rpm

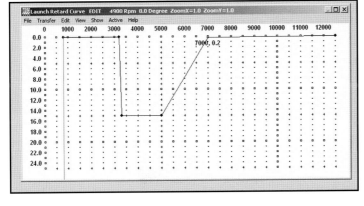

where the timing is retard 15°. It stays retarded through 5,000 rpm where it begins to ramp back to total timing by 7,000 rpm. Once the shift occurs, this timing curve is off.

Run Curve

Back to the original PN 7530. Once the car shifts, the timing switches to the run curve, the chart on the bottom. This is just like setting the mechanical advance in a distributor, but now you can modify it to handle gear change torque spikes, tire shake at certain points, or even to add a little timing at certain RPM. Advancing the timing is possible on most any timing control, but you have to reset the total timing by moving the crank trigger pickup to the advanced position. Remember, an ignition has no way of advancing the timing, it only knows what the pickup tells it! Once the overall timing is advanced, you have go to compensate for the advance at the crank trigger in the run curve and any other retard rates you program. (This will also need to be carried over into the launch curve.) Having the timing a little advanced gives you the opportunity to make very quick and very accurate, timing changes through

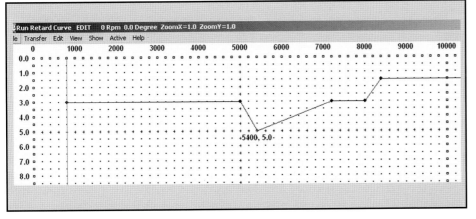

The run curve represents what the engine will be experiencing for timing through second gear and up. In this example we programmed a little high-end timing advance. This advance needs to be compensated for in all of your timing functions, including the launch, step retards, and ICM. That is why it shows a 3° retard.

the program, rather than repositioning the pickup again.

Timing requirements in the engine change as the load on the engine changes, such as in different gears and RPM as you race down the track. MSD incorporated gear retards that you can select in the menu ladder. Since you program the number of gears that your car has, the ignition keeps count of the RPM drops so it knows what gear you're in going down the track. The PN 7531 ignition takes gear curve control up a notch by providing up to six curves that can be programmed for each gear. In this ignition there is no longer a launch curve as it is now programmed for first gear. Then you map one for second gear, third gear, and so on. See, that tuning window just keeps opening wider and wider.

Individual Cylinder Timing

One area of tuning that has always posed limitations to on racers is ignition timing. Timing has always forced racers to compromise, which is not something racers like to do when it comes to performance. Timing has always been a compromise between all of the cylinders due to variances in the flow of the air/fuel mixture that occurs between combustion chambers, intake tracts, and other variables. For instance, if one or two cylinders run a little on the lean side, the result is having to set the timing a little retarded across the board just to compensate for those troubled cylinders (the bad apple syndrome).

With MSD's Programmable Ignition, as well as the Crane DEC, you can easily compensate for these cylinders with individual cylinder timing. You can program up to 10° of retard in 0.1° increments for each cylinder. To use this feature you'll need to incorporate a cam-sync signal so the ignition knows when the number one cylinder is firing to ensure that the right timing occurs in each cylinder. This encompasses installing a distributor with a separate cam-sync pickup, or fabricating a magnet in the cam gear with a pickup. Crane offers pickup kits for several different distributors and front-drive distributors. MSD created an easy way to

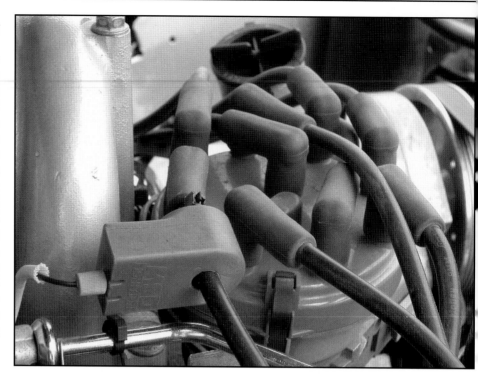

This inductive pickup will sense the number-1 cylinder firing so it can begin your individual cylinder retards. Even if the cam sync signal is lost during a run, the ignition will keep up with the correct timing order. Once the engine is shut off though, it will be gone until the cam sync is repaired.

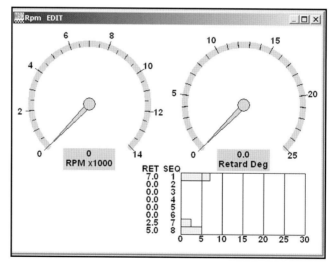

This window of the Pro-Data software will show you real-time RPM and timing retard when the PC is connected and the engine is running. The bar charts at the bottom of the screen show the individual cylinder timing. When there are other retards active they will also show up on the gauge and the bar chart.

achieve cam sync through the use of an inductive pickup. This device simply slides over the number-1 plug wire, much like a timing light pickup, and connects to the ignition through a fiber-optic cable. This lets the ignition know when the number-1 cylinder is firing so it can identify and incorporate your individual cylinder retards. Also, by using the fiber-optic cable, no EMI can interfere with this important signal.

Once the cam sync is set up, you need to go into the ignition and program the cylinders that you want retarded. But where do you start? Obviously, time on the engine dyno would be the best place to make these kinds of adjustments, but if you know your engine and check the plugs constantly, you should have a good idea on what cylinders would benefit from a little timing retard.

When setting the cylinder timing, pay close attention to the numbers on the screen, as they do not represent the cylinder numbers in the firing order. Due to the number of possibilities, MSD only lists 1-8. This means that the number two on the screen does not represent cylinder number 2 on your engine. The best thing to do is write down your firing order with 1-8 written next to them in order and have that taped to your laptop or on a note card. This is an important setting that you do not want to get confused.

Remember that any retards that are programmed for the individual cylinder management also need to be taken into consideration with all of the other retards that are programmed. All of the retards are cumulative in the MSD system for a total of 25°. If you pull 4° out of cylinder four, plus 10° on the first nitrous stage, and another 6° going down the track, the total retard is 20° in that cylinder, while only 16° in cylinders with no retard.

Step Retards

All of the ignitions that have built-in timing functions have step retards. These retards all have activation wires that need to be connected to a 12-volt signal to activate the retard. The MSD units can be used this way, plus you can also set an RPM for them to turn on at. In the menu tree under step retards there is also an RPM setting. If you program an RPM setting of 6,000 for the step-1 retard, you can connect its activation wire to a full-time 12-volt source, but the retard won't be active until the engine reaches 6,000 rpm. Note that the retard will turn off every time the engine drops below 6,000 rpm.

Another nifty feature is that you can delay the amount of time for a retard to turn off after the 12-volts signal is removed from its activation wire. This is handy when using nitrous, as the timing retard will be in effect for a set amount of time to clear any remaining traces of the gas from the engine before the timing goes back to total time. This can be adjusted in small increments under 2.5 seconds.

RPM Functions

As we mentioned about the engine load changing as you race down the track, so can the shift points. The PN 7530 lets you program a different RPM for each gear to activate a shift light. This can also be helpful if you need to short shift a couple gears, as the light can be made to come on exactly when you need to. There is also an RPM-activated window switch feature in the control that lets you activate an accessory at a selected RPM and turn it off at a different RPM. The Plus version, or 7531 as it's known, lets you select RPM, time, or even select a manifold pressure point to activate a circuit. The Crane DEC offers two timer settings. That means more options for you to ponder and experiment with. Now that you have a better understanding of some of the advanced programming options available to you, lets take a look at a few more settings that the Plus model offers.

MSD DIGITAL-7 PROGRAMMABLE PLUS

This ignition shares most of the programs we just covered. Some offer a little more control while others are completely new. The step retards of the 7531 can be activated the same way as the other ignition controls, plus they can be ramped back to total timing within 2.5 seconds. This way, the step retards won't be cumulative, since they're each ramped away. For instance, step one can be set to retard 15° and then set it to be ramped back to no retard within 0.5 second.

There are also your standard three rev limits for burnout, launch, and over-rev protection, but of course there are some racers that want another one — turbo racers specifically. These cars generally use one limit when pre-staged, then another when staged to launch. The problem is that they have trouble spooling up the turbo when preparing to do a burnout because the other limits are set at low RPM. Thus the spool limit was born.

Timing Curves

When we were reviewing the run curve of the PN 7530, we briefly mentioned that the Plus version offers a separate timing curve for each gear. First you need to select the number of gears your car has. Then you need to go to the gear retard graph and plot out what you want to accomplish in each gear. If you don't plan on changing the curve

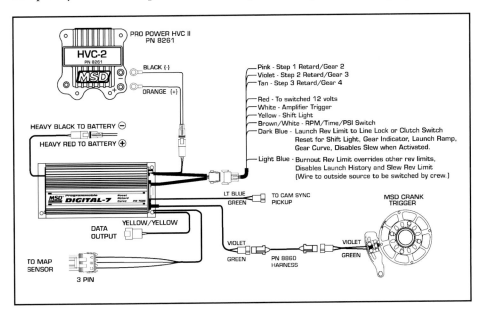

With all of the goodies included in the Programmable Digital-7 Ignition, there's really not too much to its installation. The main connections to get the engine fired are just like installing a 6AL. There are several different activation wires for the three rev limiters, RPM-activated switch, or retard steps.

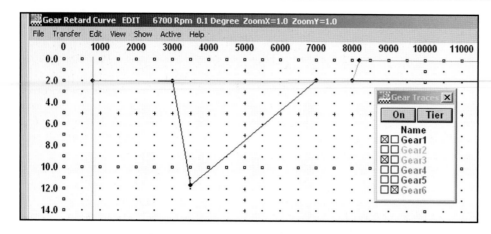

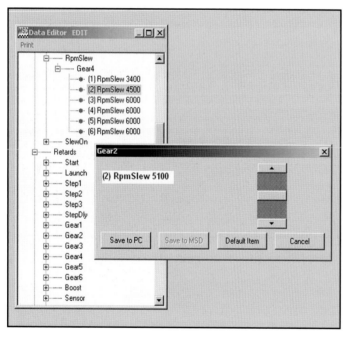

This is the gear curve chart. Each gear has its own trace and separate color (which you choose), but they're a little tough to see in black and white. The point we want to show is how first gear encompasses a lot of retard, while the other gears are copied and stacked on each other. The advance at high RPM is only programmed into fifth gear.

Setting the slew limits for each gear only takes a couple clicks of your mouse. Here we have first gear set at 3,400 rpm and we are changing the second gear value. The rest of the gears are set at 6,000 rpm. This overly simplifies setting the slew limit, as there are also other programs that need to be adjusted in order for the slew to be effective on your car.

for any gears, you'll need to copy and paste it for each gear. This derived from racers needing a first-gear-only curve, generally to help them get off the line and rolling. The middle gears are fairly constant with one another, but some of the restricted high-performance racers wanted to put a little timing back into the engine at high RPM to attempt to get a little torque back in the motor.

As if you didn't have enough curves to mess with, there's also a chart you can program based on boost/vacuum pressure. The curve can be set from 2-psia to 45-psia in 0.25-psia (pounds per square inch absolute) increments

and from 0 – 25° in 0.1° increments. To use this feature, a MAP sensor will need to be purchased (MSD offers a one 1-, 2-, and 3-Bar models).

Slew Limits

The slew-rate rev limiter is probably the most talked-about and misunderstood program in the Programmable Plus. The slew is an RPM-to-time ratio that you select to control the engine's rate of acceleration. This means that if you select 1000 rpm per second for the slew rate, it will take your engine five seconds to reach 5,000 rpm (1,000 rpm rate of acceleration per second). You

can select a different slew limit for each gear from 100 – 9,900 rpm per second. Any RPM setting is based on one second and the time is not adjustable. This ratio gives you an entirely new window for tuning and is a fresh way of trying to control tire spin going down the track (note that we did not mention anything about traction control).

The best situation is to determine your engine's ideal rate of acceleration in each gear. This is best determined through data logging and reviewing the information from several good runs. Don't have a data acquisition system? Not to worry, because the Plus ignition can record up to 20 seconds of ignition information that you can review and save on your laptop. By finding the ideal rate of acceleration, you can ensure that the tires will stay planted, because if the engine starts to accelerate too quickly, the rev limiter is activated to maintain your slew setting. Once the rate of acceleration dips below your programmed RPM, the limiter shuts off.

Setting the slew rate isn't as simple as it sounds. You need to have several ideal passes under your belt to provide you with good useable information. Plus, every car and engine is different and reacts differently going down the track. To make up for these variances, MSD had to program a couple different settings into the slew program. These include a target variance in RPM, and a high and low margin to compensate for crankshaft flexing and sharp timing variances between firings. There's more to this than meets the eye.

MSD stressed that this is not meant as an automatic traction control, as there are no sensor inputs telling the ignition real-time wheel or driveshaft speeds. It is meant to give racers another area to tune for consistency, especially when track conditions are anything but ideal. Think about it. If you're off in your slew program the limiter will be kicking in too soon and too often. Any time a rev limit hits, your performance is going to suffer, and that can cost you a race. If the slew is too high, the tires will break loose. Setting the slew on your car will take some testing and tuning to get it

EFI and Ignition Controllers

When you start getting into EFI systems you walk into another realm of tuning possibilities through fuel maps, RPM, ignition, and much, much more. Several of these systems are integrating ignition system outputs and calibrations as well.

The inductive distributorless gurus at Electromotive have been providing EFI systems for years and now offer a complete system that incorporates their HPX coil pack ignition system into the mix. These systems, called the Total Engine Control 3 (TEC3), are available for a variety of engine platforms and applications.

The TEC3 is programmable through their WinTEC software, which is Windows based, complete with easy-to-follow pull-down menus and clear screens that are easy to navigate and tune. This EFI/ignition system has data acquisition capabilities that allow you to overlay screens and graphs to compare different passes.

Electromotive offers complete EFI systems that include their accurate and high-output DIS ignition system. These systems, called the TEC3, give you an infinite number of areas to tune for the most performance. This kit is for Honda engines.

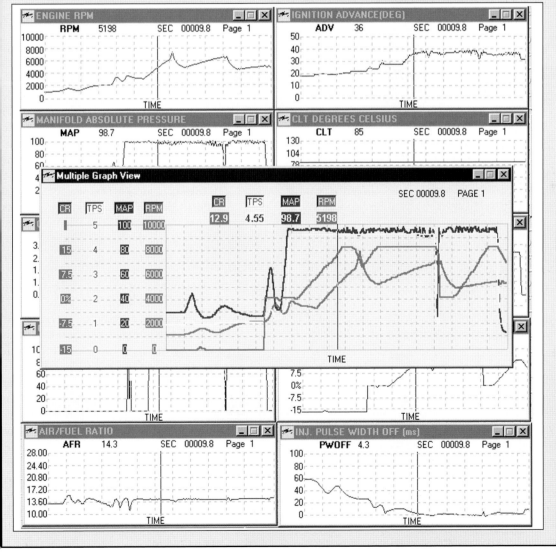

Here is a sample window of the WinTEC software from Electromotive's TEC3 EFI system. The program provides a Tuning Wizard that will get the engine fired up with minimal inputs. Then you can tune the engine on the fly to get it dialed in.

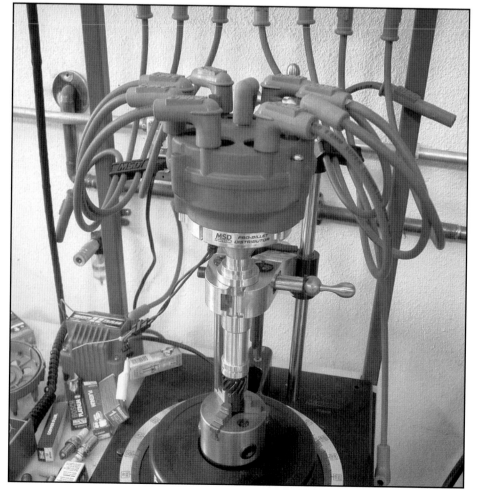

Obviously, the best place to spend time tuning your new advanced ignition system is on an engine dyno. Of course, the conditions will change dramatically when you are racing down the strip, but a dyno will let you set a good starting point to work from.

right, just like learning the clutch set-up or the fuel maps on an EFI car.

There's a closer look at the computer-programmable features that are available at this time. With the way technology continues to progress, there will probably be other programmable ignitions and features available after this book is printed. Actually, that gives us a good reason to plan a revision in a few years! Until then, you'll need to keep up with the progress of these ignitions by checking in with the companies involved, going to races, and keeping your ears open to what's going on in your racing class.

MECHANICAL PROGRAMMING

Since we just showed all of the benefits you can receive through advanced electronic tuning, what about engines that are regulated to mechanical distributors and no modern electronics? Specifically, we're talking about high-end speedway and road racing applications such as NASCAR and other circle track series. In Chapter 8, we hinted about how you can modify a billet reluctor to slightly affect when a cylinder is triggered. There are also other models out there that give you this ability.

Crane's high-performance dual optical-output distributor uses a trigger disk that has eight window openings that alternately transmit or block the infrared light. The trigger event occurs when the light goes from being blocked to being open when the window passes in front of the beam. This trigger disk

The best way to make modifications like this to a distributor is with the help of a distributor spin fixture. This way you can spin the distributor and put a timing light on each plug wire to determine the amount of timing change for each cylinder.

Using Electronics to Tune Mechanical Distributors

When you're modifying a reluctor or trigger wheel to achieve cylinder-to-cylinder timing, it will take a lot of time to learn which cylinder needs what amount of timing for the best results. Even if you have a target retard or advance for each cylinder, to get it perfect, you'll need to make an adjustment, assemble the distributor, run the engine, and then review the data. Then repeat the same procedure over and over.

A shortcut you could take would be to use one of the ignition controllers that provide individual cylinder timing. That way you can monitor and adjust each cylinder through the controller until you achieve the results you're looking for. Once you have this information, you can modify the distributor to meet these requirements and call it good!

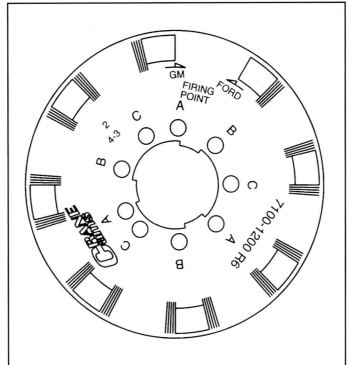

The Crane high-performance dual-trigger distributor has a trigger disk that is used to turn the trigger signal on and off. You can modify the window opening to alter the timing of certain cylinders. There are even guidelines on the disk to assist in your setup.

can be machined to advance when the window opens and even has guidelines to aid in setting up the distributor. To achieve a retard in certain cylinders, the distributor body must be moved to retard. Then you can compensate other cylinders by machining an advanced position on the disk. It is important to note that if you switch to the secondary trigger, which is 180° from the primary, the timing will be off. Therefore it is best to make timing shifts in the disk on pairs of cylinders.

The Zero-Cross Distributor from MSD is another product that came to fruition as a mechanical way to adjust individual cylinder timing. Rather than use a reluctor wheel to trigger the pickup, the distributor has eight sets of magnets that are mounted on adjustable tabs. Moving these tabs affects when each magnet set passes through the pickup, resulting in individual timing for the cylinders. Also, the primary and secondary triggers are stacked over each other so the same firing sequence occurs on both ignitions.

MSD's high-end racing distributor is called the Zero-Cross. It has individual magnetic tabs that produce a trigger signal for each cylinder. These tabs can be repositioned to provide up to 6° of timing change for every cylinder. Using a 0.010-inch feeler gauge changes the timing approximately 1° at the crankshaft.

GOING DIS
Where's the Distributor?

The distributor, as we know it, is extinct when it comes to new vehicles. It started slowly on a few cars from the early 1980s, and it really became apparent to performance enthusiasts on the turbo V6 engines of the Grand National and T-Type Buicks. The trend continued gaining momentum, and when Chevrolet put the distributor behind the water pump on the LT-1 engines, it was a sign that the distributor was on its last legs. Just a few years later (with the LS-1 engine) they were gone. For Blue Oval fans, the introduction of the Modular motor brought two coil packs to the front on the engine instead of the familiar TFI distributor. Surprisingly, most Honda engines retained distributors until the 21st century! There are probably a handful of engines that still rely on a distributor to get the spark to the spark plugs, but their time is running out.

What does this mean for performance enthusiasts? There are more electronics involved with DIS (distributorless ignition systems), but there are already performance ignition components available for many of them. Before we get into that, lets look at why the distributor became obsolete, the benefits of DIS, and how the system operates.

A distributor shaft spins by being connected to the camshaft through helically cut gears. One of these gears is turned by the camshaft, which is rotated through another set of gears joined by a chain to the crankshaft. This is a long chain of mechanical meshing and turning, which means there is bound to be inefficiencies. Now, put all of these components under the load of full throttle, and any variables that were minute at idle or moderate speeds are now becoming a factor. The mechanical flexing and twisting, varying frequencies, and the pistons pounding down on the crank, can all add up to timing variations.

Wrong place, wrong time. You won't find a distributor on most engines any more. They've been replaced with sophisticated coil-per-cylinder, coil-on-plug, or coil-pack ignition systems. This HEI has no business being near Chevrolet's LS-1 engine, which has a coil for each cylinder.

Going DIS means there are no more caps and rotors to wear or replace. Most DIS systems incorporate spark plug wires, but there are factory systems that now put the coil right on top of the spark plug.

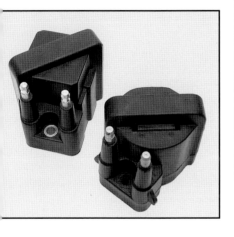

GM used these two-tower coil packs since the mid 1980s to fire many of their 4- and 6-cylinder engines. Many companies offer replacement performance models for this style of coil.

This is a coil pack on a Ford Modular engine from about 1996. The coil pack has four towers, with two channels. This means two towers fire at the same time, while one cylinder is on the compression stroke and the other is on the exhaust stroke.

Plus, as engine component technology has progressed, the RPM that race engines run and live through has also risen. These extra RPM have brought out slight timing gremlins that didn't necessarily come into play a few years ago. High RPM brings out the worst in a distributor that is responsible for triggering the ignition. This is one reason most that most high-end race cars trigger the ignition with a crank trigger system. It was just within the last few years that Top Fuel Dragsters incorporated crank triggers to fire their magnetos. This brought terrific results, with very steady timing signals compared to having the trigger inside the generator. But it wasn't really a fault in the distributor

that brought about its demise, it was electronics!

As OEMs moved to using more and more electronic controls, the distributor first lost its timing control functions to electronic spark timing. The next thing that went was its responsibility of supplying the trigger signals, since crank sensors could provide a more accurate signal. This left the distributor doing just that, distributing the sparks from the all-new electronic ignition system. This mechanical operation is really quite a feat considering that the different components must all work in unity. Since the ignition was being fired from a crank sensor, and the advanced electronics in the ignition module were controlling the dwell and spark delivery, it certainly made sense to do away with the distributor completely. This was accomplished by incorporating

multiple coil packs to step up the voltage and distribute it to the spark plugs. Welcome to distributorless ignition technology.

As with all things automotive, there are a few different versions of DIS ignitions used, though they all work in much the same way. There are systems with coil packs that fire two cylinders at once. One cylinder is under compression, while its opposite cylinder is on the exhaust stroke. This design is referred to as a waste-spark system. You'd think that it would take away from the coil's output by firing two cylinders, but remember that one cylinder is on the exhaust stroke, so there is no cylinder pressure. This means that it doesn't take much voltage at all to jump the plug gap. Even though two cylinders are getting fired, there is plenty of punch in the coil pack and the spark.

Engines with dual-tower coils packs can still get the benefits of a multiple sparking CD ignition control. The Fireball HI-6DI2 is like having two HI-6 ignitions in one box. This unit has two ignition outputs to drive two separate dual-tower coil packs.

This LS-1 Chevy engine uses a coil for each cylinder. Replacing these coils for higher-output performance models is tough because the transistors that monitor the firing are built into each coil. This means you can't just swap out the coil for any replacement.

In recent years the OEMs have been using ignition systems with individual coils per cylinder. If you have an 8-cylinder engine, there's going to be eight coils. There are four coils for 4-cylinder engines, and so on and so forth. You wouldn't think this would be a money-saving upgrade for the big guys, since they're now buying several times as many coils as before. The coils are much smaller, since they only fire one time for every complete engine cycle and there is plenty of time to charge each coil. And we already know that this means a hotter spark through higher RPM. All this adds up to improved performance and economy, which is exactly why you're seeing more of these systems.

Coil Pack Ignition Upgrades

Since coil pack DIS ignition technology has been available for over a decade, most of the aftermarket now offers different components and accessories. The most common ignition upgrade, just like a distributor ignition, is a CD ignition control. Crane and MSD both offer ignition controls that are designed just like their regular ignition controls.

The Crane Fireball HI-6DI2 ignition control is one answer for engines with two dual-tower coil packs. This ignition delivers multiple high-voltage capacitive discharge sparks, just like its sibling HI-6 series ignitions. The dif-

This wiring diagram shows the installation of the HI-6DI2 to a 1990 Mitsubishi. Note that a Tach Adapter is required in this installation to generate a high-voltage signal that will trigger both the EFI and the Crane ignition. Depending on your application, two adapters may be required.

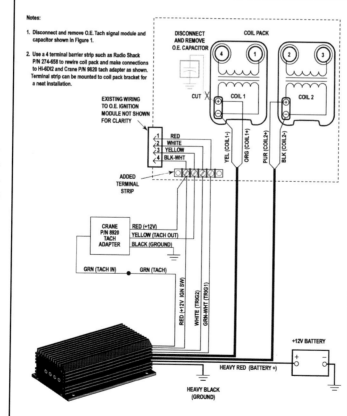

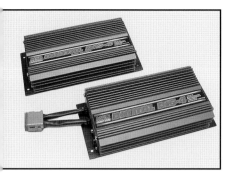

If you have three or four coil packs that are in need of the multiple-spark power of a CD ignition, MSD has one that's up to the task. The DIS-4 will deliver high-voltage, full power sparks to four different coil packs. A race-only version is also available as the DIS-4 HO (for High Output).

...erence is that the DI2 has two ignition outputs, so it can fire both two-tower coils on a 4-cylinder engine. It even delivers two adjustable rev limiters, so you'll have an over-rev RPM limit and a staging limit. This is a great addition for Mitsubishi Eclipses, Eagle Talons, and Dodge Neons. If you're running nitrous or adding a forced-induction system, Crane's TRC-2 retard control can easily be wired into the system.

The installation of these units is even similar to that of a single channel distributor triggered ignition. There are two sets of coil primary wires (outputs) and two input wires that intercept the ECU's trigger signal. Of course there are the supply wires that connect to the battery positive and negative terminals and one on/off wire. The installation is not complicated, but it is recommended to have the wiring diagram for your vehicle so you know for sure which color wire does what function. Just like the distributor-fired ignitions, there is the chance that a tach adapter or possibly two will be needed for the factory tach and the EFI to function properly.

MSD Ignition also offers a line of multi-channel ignition controls for distributorless ignitions with coil packs. They offer the MSD DIS-4, which is a four-channel ignition control. This unit can be used on 6-cylinder engines with three coil packs and on 8-cylinder engines with four coil packs. You could really even use it on a 4-cylinder with

More Adjustment

So you have your DIS-4 ignition system on your car, but you just have to have more control and tuning ability? MSD offers a couple different multi-channel ignition controllers that give you plenty.

These controllers are similar to the add-on controls that we discussed in Chapters 8 and 9. The units wire into your existing DIS-ignition and allow you to interface your laptop into the ignition tuning. If you need to retard the timing in relation to boost pressure you could map out an entire curve based on manifold pressure. There's even a launch retard rate that allows you to pull timing out during the holeshot to aid in reducing tire spin.

There is also another version available with a fuel adder feature. The unit will drive up to four additional fuel injectors to increase the fuel delivery by up to 50%. This provides a unique opportunity to add fuel to the mix for engines that have been heavily modified and are being force-fed a lot of boost pressure.

The Programmable Multi-Channel Boost Controller plugs into the MSD DIS series ignition controls to give you lap top programming capabilities through the ignition. The unit comes MSD's Pro-Data+ software program for Windows based PCs.

two coil packs, but you'd be spending extra money on two channels that you wouldn't even use. For these applications, they also offer a two-channel version called the DIS-2. The unit also provides top-end and holeshot rev limiters that are adjustable with built-in dip switches.

One of the first late-model muscle engines to go distributorless was the Buick turbo V6. This engine used a single coil-pack assembly that consisted of three dual-tower coil packs. The challenge to wiring an MSD DIS-4 into this system is that the coil pack sits right against the ignition module. MSD offers an interface module for the sought-after intercooled 1986 and 1987 models that sandwiches between the coil packs and the ignition module and connects the coils directly to the DIS-4 unit. They also offer a similar interface to use on GM's popular twin-tower coil packs.

These ignitions will fit most engines that use coil packs in waste-spark systems. They're not intended for ignitions

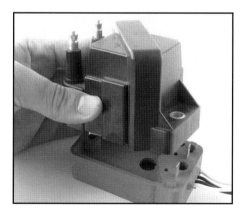

Simply remove the two screws that hold the coil pack to the module, lift the coil out, sit the MSD Interface on the module, and reinstall the coil pack. These interfaces separate the 12-volt and trigger terminals of the ignition module from the primary coil terminals. That way you can easily install the MSD ignition.

with one coil per cylinder, though we've seen it a couple times on engines that have had their electrical systems modified. If you're looking for improved coil

The Programmable DIS-2 delivers multiple high-voltage sparks while letting you tune in the complete ignition system from rev limits to retarts that activate when you shift. It is designed for 4-cylinder engines with two coil packs and it is for drag race applications only.

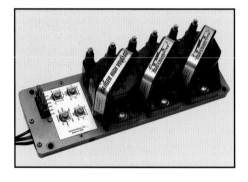

This is the Electromotive HPX system for a 6-cylinder engine, as noted by the three dual-tower coil packs. The HPX's internal circuitry receives angular based crank info from a 60-tooth trigger wheel that you mount to the balancer. This way the ignition knows exactly how much the crank has traveled to aid its coil charging circuits.

output, you can always wire two single-tower coils together in series so the system still has its waste spark capabilities. This can be done by connecting a wire between a coil's negative terminal to the other coil's positive terminal. The ignition's primary wires for that channel would go to the first coil's positive post and the negative wire to the second coil's negative terminal. If you have any questions about your car's compatibility, drop

the ignition companies a line through their email and ask them directly!

PROGRAMMABLE DIS IGNITION CONTROLS

If you have a race engine with a dual coil pack ignition and need to be able to control every aspect of the ignition to dial in your car's performance, the Programmable DIS-2 could be just what you needed.

The Programmable unit is a cross between MSD's Digital Programmable 7 Ignition and their DIS-2 ignition. The result is a programmable DIS-2 that lets you set a holeshot, burnout, and top-end rev limit, multi-step retards, cylinder timing, a boost timing curve, and much more. For detailed programming information, go to Chapter 9. Since this unit is designed with serious racing in mind, its output was boosted over that of the street-legal DIS units. The trade-off is that the ignition is only recommended for short duration racing use, depending on which coils you use with it. The stock coils will only be able to handle short events like drag racing, where as a better CD coil could handle longer racing events. You won't be making any road trips with this ignition tied into the system though.

ELECTROMOTIVE

One company that was and still is ahead of the DIS game is Electromotive. This company specializes in converting most any engine to a distributorless ignition system and has been doing this since the early 1980s. In fact, they hold several important patents regarding DIS operation and coil charging. So if you're ready to dump that old distributor entirely, Electromotive's HPX may be the system for you.

We first brought up the Electromotive ignition system in Chapter 3 when we were discussing inductive ignition systems. Remember that these ignitions are inductive designs. Since there is one coil for every two cylinders, the charge time of each coil can be four times that of a distributor-triggered ignition. This means that the ignition has no trouble

These are the adjustment knobs on the HPX ignition. Just like the other ignition controls and accessories we've mentioned, you can set an ignition curve, two-step rev limiters, and even wire in a retard step for nitrous.

producing full-output sparks to well over racing RPM. Plus, the spark duration is extended thanks to the inductive firing characteristics of an inductive ignition design.

The HPX system is easy to install on most any traditional engine with a distributor. If you are really lacking firewall clearance, or you simply want to get away from the gear-driven trigger mechanism and distribution of a distributor, Electromotive tries to make it easy on you. Their system uses a crank trigger to provide the HPX with trigger information. Unlike the crank trigger systems we discussed earlier, the HPX uses a wheel with 60 teeth (okay, 58, due to the flat area indicating a complete revolution to the computer) with a magnetic pickup. The extra teeth trigger the pickup and provide the added information so ignition knows the location and angle of the crankshaft throughout every revolution. This means that the HPX can make firing and rev limiting compensations, plus this aids in precision charging of the each coil pack.

When GM and Ford started going with DIS systems, they turned to Electromotive's patented technology for their technique in charging multiple inductive coils. Now, these factory systems are licensed from Electromotive, though the factory doesn't use them to the capacity they're capable of delivering. We suspect that's all right at the

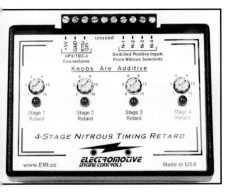

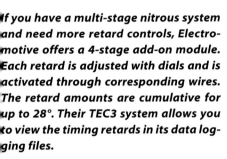

If you have a multi-stage nitrous system and need more retard controls, Electromotive offers a 4-stage add-on module. Each retard is adjusted with dials and is activated through corresponding wires. The retard amounts are cumulative for up to 28°. Their TEC3 system allows you to view the timing retards in its data logging files.

The newer TEC3 system provides full fuel and ignition programming to your car. The distributorless ignition system portion of the TEC3 has a long list of performance programming ignition accessories, such as three rev limits, step retards, and data acquisition features. The system shown is for Ford's Modular engines.

If you have a V8, you can power eight coils with MSD's CPC digital ignition system. This system still uses capacitive discharge technology with multiple sparks to each coil. The system can be used on 6- and 8-cylinder engines.

Electromotive offices, so they can continue to offer higher-output performance components.

The latest step in these inductive coil-pack systems combine EFI management through what they call Total Engine Control with their TEC3 system. This system combines detailed fuel control with their inductive DIS system. You can either create your own EFI system, or the TEC3 can be installed on a late-model car such as an LS-1 powered Camaro. In this case, the TEC3 can be wired to where it takes over the factory fuel controls and ignition duties from the factory ECU. The stock computer must be retained for things such as trans shifts, body controls, and other features. The two systems will even share some of the same sensors but the fuel mapping and ignition programs will be at your fingertips to tweak and modify. For many late model vehicles, this is the only system that can provide you with the ability to program and modify the ignition system.

We mentioned there were benefits to an inductive system, and spark duration is the biggest one. With a coil pack ignition system like the HPX, an inductive system has time to charge each coil pack between firings so you can take advantage of the lengthy duration. Elec-

tromotive offers performance enthusiasts a different way to think about ignition systems and inductive ignitions in particular. They offer a variety different trigger wheels and accessories to make installing an HPX easy with only three wires to connect. The one thing you'll need to buy separately for sure is a set of plug wires!

CPC IGNITION SYSTEM

As we mentioned earlier in this chapter, OEM's have been incorporating ignitions that are using a coil for every cylinder. This gives each coil plenty of time to be thoroughly charged and ready to fire. There are certainly benefits to going to a distributorless or even an individual-coil-per-cylinder (CPC) system, but what about for the carbureted group that are looking for something even more different than a coil pack distributorless system? How about an aftermarket ignition that that uses a coil per cylinder?

MSD introduced their Coil-Per-Cylinder (CPC) system a couple years ago. It can be used to with carbs or with EFI, but it is not a replacement kit for a late-model car. There are two control boxes that make up the system. One is a digital control unit that handles all the timing and RPM controls, while the

The MSD CPC has two control boxes that can be mounted together or away from each other with a harness extension. The system does take up some real estate, but the accurate timing and improved spark delivery should make it all worthwhile.

other is the ignition power unit that creates the high-voltage CD sparks and gets them to the coil packs. Like many of MSD's latest offerings, the ignition is programmable from a PC or laptop.

A crank trigger system must be installed to provide the ignition with accurate trigger signals. Since this kit is meant to replace distributors, a distributor plug is required to drive the oil pump. This shaft spins at camshaft speed, so MSD incorporated a Hall-effect switch on top of the housing to supply the ignition with a cam sync signal. That way, it knows when each cylinder is firing and can keep the engine firing in the correct order.

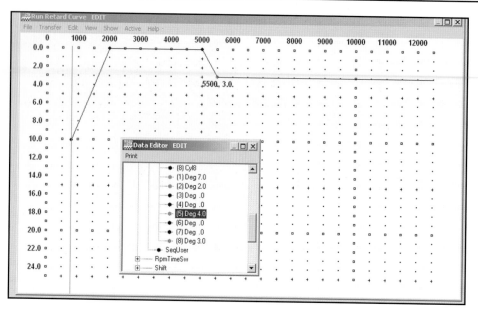

This is a capture of the MSD software for their CPC system. We zoomed in on the individual cylinder timing rates and the ignition run curve, which is similar to what you would set the mechanical advance of a distributor to achieve. Only this time, you can make adjustments in seconds without getting your hands dirty.

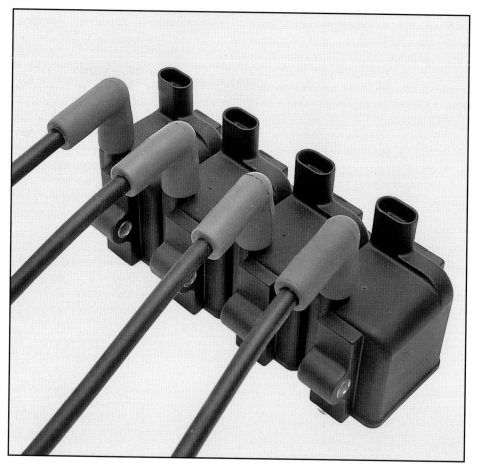

One thing that these different distributorless systems all require is spark plug wires. However, as technology continues to advance with more advanced distributorless systems and coils, perhaps their days, like those of the distributor, are numbered.

The CPC system comes with the controls and their wiring. Also, since there are different balancers, engine sizes, and makes, you need to purchase the coils, crank trigger kit, and spark plug wires separately. A coil harness will also need to be chosen since there are different firing orders on different engines. It all adds up to a pretty hefty sum, but there are advantages to the programming and the individual coils. Once everything is mounted and you fire up the engine for the first time, the next step will be tweaking the tune-up here and there.

The software lets you select three different rev limits, four retard stages, different activation points for a shift light, and other little things. The big item that can be adjusted is of course, the cylinder-to-cylinder timing. This way you don't need to compromise all the cylinders to make up for just one that requires a couple degrees of retard. Another great feature is a boost timing curve and a launch curve that can be advantageous to cars limited to small tires.

There are the three different examples of distributorless ignition systems, and you can bet that more are coming. As more people get comfortable with all those coils and the programming, you'll see more coil-per-cylinder systems at the track and on the street. There will probably be more versions available from other companies as well, which will peak even more interest. Some companies are taking their advance ignition controlling technology and intertwining it with their own fuel-injection systems like Electromotive. Other companies are taking their EFI controlling systems and adding more ignition programming features as well as drivers for coil packs. MoTeC is known for their EFI programming capabilities on race engines around the world, and they have been adding more and more ignition tuning functions and spark controls to their ECU controllers.

One thing for certain is that distributorless ignitions are not going to go away any time soon. Could the next thing be a coil-on-plug ignition from the aftermarket? It wouldn't surprise us at all.

CHARGING AND WIRING
Batteries, Alternators, and Wiring

We've covered all the parts and components necessary to produce a high-performance ignition system. There is, however, one other system on your car that dictates how the ignition performs — the charging system. This system includes the battery that provides a reserve of voltage and current for use to start the engine, and the alternator that continuously creates the current needed for all of your car's electrical systems. Without these parts, your ignition system will just sit there and look pretty. (That is of course, unless you use a magneto.)

BATTERIES

The battery of your car is like a fuel tank full of electricity. It is there to get the car running by powering the starter and ignition, or other components such as the fuel pump and EFI system. Once the engine fires up, the charging system takes over the supply chores, and unless there are moments when it can't keep up, the battery sits in wait unit it's called upon again.

For street cars, a battery is really only going to come into play when you start the car, or if you're parked with the engine off listening to the radio. An important specification to look for here is cold cranking amps. This determines the amount of current that the battery

can deliver for 30 seconds at 0°F. Most of us aren't worried about how our performance car will crank at these Antarctic conditions, but we are worried about how they'll crank after a hot soak on a hot summer night cruise. If you have a high compression, big cubic-inch engine, go with a high-grade battery with 800 or more cold cranking amps.

Another rating you'll see on batteries is the reserve capacity rating. This is the time needed to lower the battery

voltage from a fully charged state to below 10.2 volts with a draw of 25 amps. This is important on race cars that don't use an alternator, as it represents how long a battery will deliver voltage above 10.2 volts.

Also, for street rods where mounting the battery can require some creativity, a dry cell battery is a good idea. Since there's no acid or liquid in these batteries, they can be mounted in any position.

There are a lot of choices when it comes to a battery and charging system. Things you need to consider are your application and the current draw of the electrical components you are running during a race.

A dry-cell battery has no liquid acid or gels inside, which means it can be mounted in most any manner you need. Plus, in the event of an accident, there is no acid to leak out. This Holley Annihilator battery is compact for weight savings, plus it has high cranking power.

There are many batteries available ranging from 12 to 16 and even 18 volts and racers use them all in different ways. The most common is to use dual batteries connected in parallel. This way, you still operate with a 12-volt system, but gain extra capacity with two batteries. We've also heard about some crafty racers connecting two smaller 8-volt tractor type batteries in series to save weight over dual 12-volt systems.

The benefit of running dual 12 or 16-volt batteries is reserve capacity. If there is one thing that racers don't agree on, it's whether or not they need a high-voltage battery or dual batteries. Some racers don't even bother with an alternator in drag racing or short-duration circle track events. It all comes down to knowing what your car's electrical system needs to get through a race without falling off in electrical output.

You may hear about starting batteries and deep-cycle batteries. Starting batteries are designed for just that, providing the go-juice for the starter, ignition, and EFI system. Once the alternator kicks in, the battery sits back and relaxes for the most part. Deep cycle batteries are designed to handle being charged and fully discharged over and over again. If you don't run an alternator, you may be leaning towards going with the deep-cycle battery; however, many

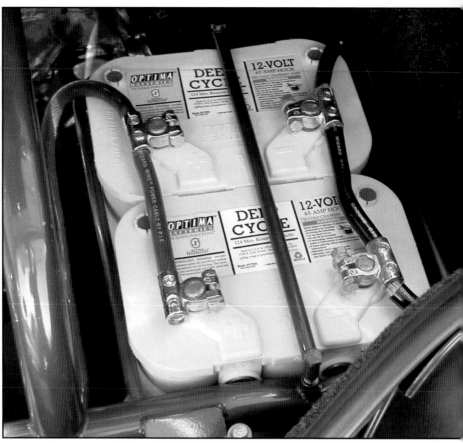

When you connect two batteries in parallel (positive to positive and negative to negative), you retain the 12-volt output, but gain the extra reserve capacity of the extra battery. That way, you can maintain a useable output to the electrical components on the car. Two identical batteries should be used if you're running them in parallel.

of these are not designed to take the brunt of a between-round, high-current mega charge. Most deep cycle batteries like a longer low-current charge. It's best to ask the manufacturer to match a battery to your specifications.

16-Volt Batteries

Batteries that maintain and deliver 16 volts are common on racing applications. Turbostart is well known for their 16-volt battery technology, and they offer a variety of different batteries. The main benefit here is extra capacity. Most 12-volt batteries will have a full charge of 12.6 volts, while a Turbostart will have 16.8 volts. This extra capacity is especially important on race engines that do not incorporate a charging system.

It is interesting to note that stepping up to a 16-volt system does not improve the output of a capacitive discharge ignition control. Most CD igni-

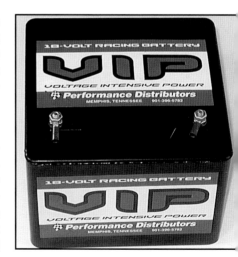

Performance Distributors offers an 18-volt battery called the Voltage Intensive Power (VIP). It is designed for race cars using their Dyna-Module and DUI Coil without an alternator. It is only meant to power the ignition, not crank the engine.

tions will clamp down their supply voltage to fit their needs and let their transformer step up the voltage. However, a CD ignition's output will suffer if the battery voltage begins to drop below 11 volts or so. An inductive ignition on the other hand, such as the GM HEI, will definitely enjoy the benefits of receiving 16 volts. Remember, an inductive ignition uses the battery voltage to charge the coil, so a little more voltage is a good thing with inductive systems. Both systems will benefit from the added capacity that a 16-volt battery supplies.

Battery Charging Tips

Just about every racer puts a charge on the battery between heats or passes down the strip. Here's a few tips and precautions, especially with a 16-volt charger.

- When charging the battery between rounds, always have the system disconnect switch turned off. This will prevent other components from being damaged due to the increased voltage of the charger.
- Do not start the car with the charger connected. Once again, the excess voltage could feed through your car's electrical system and damage components.
- Don't try to print out race data information from the car with the charger connected.
- If you have any question about a component's ability to handle 16 volts, contact the manufacturer.

CHARGING SYSTEM

Unless you're in a flat-out drag car, you're going to need an alternator to keep the battery charged and provide the voltage and current to the rest of the car. The battery provides its energy to get the car fired up, but once the engine is running, the charging system is responsible for keeping the electrons flowing while maintaining a charge on the battery.

There are two types of charging components that you'll hear about: a generator and an alternator. Generators

Choosing an alternator that meets your car's charging needs is imperative. If your car exceeds the output of the charging system, the performance of the ignition, fuel pumps, and other electrical components will suffer.

were used on older cars when there wasn't a high demand for current output. A generator is defined as creating a direct current (DC) current, like an electric motor. The output conductor windings, called the armature, spins inside a stationary magnetic field. The current is induced from the field into the armature, where a direct current is created and used. Generators were limited in their output, especially at low RPM where they were very inefficient.

An alternator is really a generator that produces an alternating current (AC) that flows both directions. The big difference is in its construction, as the magnets that produce the magnetic field are connected to the rotor and spin inside the stationary stator assembly. This field is induced into the stator's windings that surround the rotor to achieve a very efficient build up of current.

The trouble here is that the electrical systems on cars are designed for direct current only! This problem is rectified, so to speak, through a series of diodes called a rectifier circuit. It controls the current flow to one useable

This is an external regulator on a '65 Pontiac. Since a one-wire alternator with an internal regulator has been installed, the stock regulator is not a part of the charging system anymore. It does help retain the stock appearance of a restored muscle car though.

What's the Deal With One Wire?

The XS Volt one-wire alternator from PowerMaster can be adjusted for use on 12 or 16-volt systems. There is a potentiometer on the back of the housing, so if you move up to a 16-volt system on your race car, you won't have to change the alternator.

Most of the performance alternators available today feature a one-wire connection between the battery and alternator. Some models can be used both ways. The biggest difference is how the alternator turns on. With an OEM-style connection, the alternator is turned on through the ignition switch. One-wire alternators have an internal sensing circuit that wakes up the alternator once it hits a certain RPM. This means that when you start the car, it will not be charging until the engine is revved over a certain RPM, generally 1,200 – 1,400 rpm and even more on higher output models. Once the alternator is activated, it will charge at low RPM as well.

Installing a one-wire alternator is easy as, well, all you need to connect is one wire between the battery and the alternator. Racing alternators obviously require thicker gauge wire, and the length of the wire also needs to be taken into consideration. If your car had an external regulator, you'll need to disconnect it to prevent the dash light indicator from staying on.

Some racers like to switch the alternator off throughout a race, but this is not recommended with one-wire alternators. Switching it off will result in severe internal spikes, resulting in damage.

Having only one wire leading to the alternator means less wiring, fewer connections, and fewer chances for problems to arise. For the neat-street freaks, it also provides a tidier appearance. The one thing you'll need to do is rev the engine over 1,200 rpm or so to activate the charging.

between the battery and the rotor windings. Most regulators are inside the alternators, but older cars may have external voltage regulators mounted to the firewall or radiator support.

Choosing an Alternator

There are several things that need to be considered when choosing an alternator, the most important being the current draw from the components on your car. The best thing to do is to add up all the electrical components that sap up current. Most of these specifications can be found with the manufacturers, but to give you an idea, a typical drag race ignition uses one amp per 1,000 rpm, nitrous solenoids can pull up to 15 amps, water and fuel pumps another 15 or more each, and don't forget all those thumping stereo amps that can put a pretty hefty drain on the system. Once you have a good idea of the kind of current your car is eating up you, need to consider the mounting location, as well as the pulley diameter.

Pulleys

When you're setting up the alternator for your race car, the pulley choice is very important. The output of an alternator is dependent on the speed at which it is driven, which is determined

RECOMMENDED CHARGING CABLE GAUGE SIZE

AMPS	UP TO 4'	4'–7'	7'–10'	10'–13'	13'–16'	16'–19'	19'–22'	22'–28'
35-50	12	12	10	10	10	8	8	8
50-65	10	10	8	8	6	6	6	4
65-85	10	8	8	6	6	4	4	4
85-105	8	8	6	4	4	4	4	2
105-125	6	6	4	4	2	2	2	0
125-150	6	6	4	2	2	2	2	0
150-175	4	4	4	2	2	0	0	0
175-200	4	4	2	2	0	0	0	00

The charge wire between the alternator and the battery is not a place to skimp on size. Also, the length of the wire should determine the gauge size as well. This chart shows some recommended wire samples.

direction, thus changing it into DC current. This is sometimes referred to as a diode trio and is responsible for changing the AC current to DC for use throughout the car.

Another important part of the alternator and charging circuit is the voltage regulator. The regulator watches over the charging system and determines if more or less output is needed by sensing the voltage in the system. Then it controls the amount that goes into the rotor windings to increase the output and will limit output by adding resistance

If you're trying to maintain a stock-type appearance, an ignition control can usually be installed somewhere to make it inconspicuous. This Crane unit is tucked away in the fender well. Rev limits won't be easy to adjust, but this shouldn't present a problem for street cars.

Pulley selection is imperative to the operation of your charging system. For circle track racing, a good rule of thumb ratio is 1:1 between the engine and the pulley. Drag racers will want to overdrive the pulley, so 1.75:1 is recommended. Street cars should shoot for about 3:1.

by its pulley size. This is important to match to the average RPM that the engine experiences, because an alternator's output is not linear. Its speed makes a big difference in its output.

To determine the alternator to engine pulley ratio, divide the diameter of the crankshaft pulley by the diameter of the alternator's pulley. Once you know the ratio, you can determine the RPM that the alternator is spinning by multiplying the ratio by the engine RPM. For example, if you determine the ratio to be 2.1:1, at 2,800 rpm the alternator will be spinning at 5,880 rpm. This sounds like a lot of RPM, but most performance alternators are capable of handling upwards of 20,000 rpm for

short durations, so overdriving the pulley should not present any troubles.

WIRING TIPS

Wiring demands patience! Even making a set of plug wires can be time consuming when you take the time to carefully route the wires and add heat guards or accessories. If that pushes the limits of your patience, think about wiring a complete EFI system! After that, you should feel much better about taking your time to ensure that the ignition system is wired correctly.

It is safe to say that half of the ignition system problems that occur can be traced to poor wiring. Either through

cheesy connectors, poor-quality crimps, the wrong style wiring being used, or even poorly chosen wire routing. It can all add up to headaches that may leave you pulling your hair out at the race track, or worse yet, on the side of the road.

If you have a new ignition control to install, make a plan. Thinking ahead of where all of the wiring needs to go will save you from hitting roadblocks after you start. Not only will this help when routing the wires to their connections, but it can also help suppress or prevent electro magnetic interference (EMI), which can cause even more migraines.

Most ignition controls are designed to handle under-hood conditions. If you're not worried about adjusting rev limits or doing anything where you need to access the control, you can choose to put it in an out of the way spot such as under the battery tray. Some ignition controls are potted with an epoxy compound, but some of the street models are not. If the unit is not potted, do not try to mount it upside down. Doing so would trap any moisture inside, which could present problems down the road. And being down

Vibration mounts are always a good idea to use when mounting the ignition control. Many models are supplied with a set of these heavy-duty mounts. Most companies offer these mounts separately.

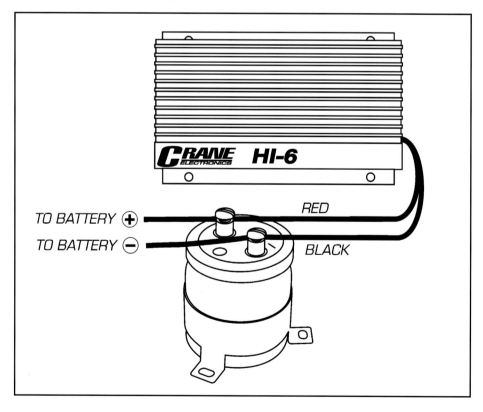

Installing a noise filter, or capacitor, on the power lines of the ignition control is never a bad addition. These act as a filter to protect the ignition against voltage and current surges, and they can even help deter supply-line radio noise.

the road when a problem occurs is not a place we want to be.

An ignition control can also be mounted in the interior of your car, such as on the cowling under the dash. Don't put the ignition in an enclosure such as the glove box as they do get quite warm and having a little air circulation over and around the area is a good idea. If you do install the ignition under the dash, it's imperative to use rubber grommets to route the wires through the firewall! This is especially important with the primary coil wires since they're carrying extremely high voltages.

Once a mounting position has been chosen and the box is in place, begin routing the wires to their connectors. The best place for the ignition to be connected is directly to the battery positive terminal or from a direct junction off the positive terminal. We've seen these wires connected to the positive side of the starter solenoid but it really isn't the best place for it, since the starter pulls such a large amount of current and there are more chances of voltage spikes. Never connect the ignition's power source to the alternator wire! This can cause excessive voltage and current, either of which can damage the ignition control. Obviously, the best place for the ignition's ground is to the engine block itself, or to the battery's negative terminal.

Once the power supply wires are connected, you can move on to routing the other wires. The coil primary leads are important connections to say the least. Remember that these wires can have over 500 volts pulsing through them! It is best if you keep these wires routed separately from the trigger pickup wires to reduce the chance of interference. When you're deciding on a coil mounting location, it is better to keep the high-voltage secondary coil wire shorter than these wires, but you don't really want to have to extend these wires. If it is necessary, use a larger gauge wire for the extension or even switch the entire wire to an improved thickness. Most 6-Sereis ignitions use 18-gauge wiring, so stepping them up to 16 or even 14 gauge would be a good move. Most of the higher-output racing

You're Grounded!

Anyone that doesn't take the time to properly ground their ignition system should be the one that gets grounded. Poor electrical grounds can and will result in inconsistencies and erratic performance on race cars and will definitely lead to intermittent problems on the street. The ground path is just as important as the positive power source wire, so make sure the ground wiring and paths are up to snuff.

Most racers will simply connect the battery ground to the chassis, and then run ground straps from the engine to the chassis. This works, but the best ground path you can create is to run a high-grade copper battery cable straight from the battery negative terminal to the engine block. Even if your battery is mounted in the trunk, the assurance of having this ground will be worth the extra work and minor cost of a few more feet of wiring. Having the battery grounded right to the engine block just can't be beat. From there you can run a heavy-duty wire to the chassis and connect other electrical grounds.

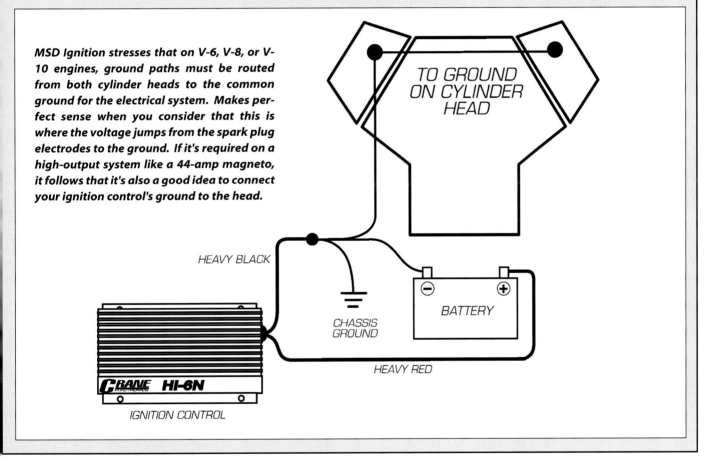

MSD Ignition stresses that on V-6, V-8, or V-10 engines, ground paths must be routed from both cylinder heads to the common ground for the electrical system. Makes perfect sense when you consider that this is where the voltage jumps from the spark plug electrodes to the ground. If it's required on a high-output system like a 44-amp magneto, it follows that it's also a good idea to connect your ignition control's ground to the head.

ignitions incorporate 14-guage wire on their primary leads already.

Routing the Trigger Wires

Keeping the magnetic pickup wires separate and confined from other wiring is something you should definitely strive to achieve. These wires are carrying a voltage signal to tell the ignition when to fire, so you do not want other wiring inducing their voltage into the trigger wires. These wires should be twisted together to help produce a choke to keep EMI from coming into play. They should be routed separately and it is best to run them right along the frame or engine for a ground plain to help isolate their signal. As more electronics are used in racing applications such as EFI systems, data acquisition, and retard controls, there is more of a chance of interference occurring. The best thing you can do to protect the trigger wires is to use a shielded cable that protects the wires through a grounded shield.

Wire Connections

Race cars are taken apart a lot and that can put quite a strain on your wiring connections. This makes it important to use high-quality connectors that can be opened and closed hun-

Disconnect Switch

When you're drag racing, you'll need an externally operated switch that will kill the power through the entire car. If you're racing around in circles, a main kill switch needs to be mounted within reach of the driver inside the car. Also, having one on your street car is not a bad idea as a theft deterrent. Mostly though, these disconnect switches are for race cars.

NHRA mandates that the switch be installed on the main positive wire of the battery and must be capable of shutting off all electrical functions, including the ignition, fuel pumps, fans, etc. The switch must be mounted on the back of the car and the off position must clearly be labeled. If you use a push/pull method, the push motion must shut the system off.

If you have a street car and prefer to keep a stealthy appearance when you're not on the strip, you can install the kill switch inside the trunk positioned so it toggles forward to turn off

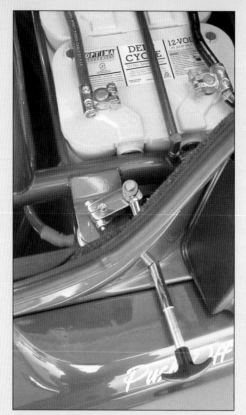

and towards the rear to turn on. Then, install a removable steel rod through to the outside of the car that can be pushed to kill the power. When you're not racing, you can remove the rod and no one will be the wiser, except you'll have "push off" written on the back of the car.

If you have a trunk-mounted battery, you'll need a main disconnect switch that will shut off power to the entire car (make sure you have a mechanical, not electric, trunk release!). Moroso offers a super-duty disconnect switch that can handle up to 300 continuous amps, plus it has two studs for connecting electrical components.

On racing applications, mounting the coil closer to the distributor is always recommended. For street rods or cars that put the coil under the dash, a firewall feed-through is a good idea. These mount to the firewall and provide the added isolation needed to protect the coil wire.

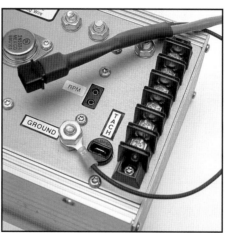

A shielded magnetic pickup cable has a braided piece of wire that surrounds the signal wires. This braided wire gets grounded on one side, generally at the ignition control. This ground will effectively shield any voltage noise from other components before they could interfere with the pickup signals.

Using high-quality, locking, sealed connectors is the only way to go when it comes to ignition components, or any wiring for that matter. Two popular connectors used in ignition wiring are the black Weatherpak-style connecter and the gray Deutsch connectors.

dreds of times and still provide a locked and sealed connection.

Two of the most common connectors used in ignition wiring are Weatherpak connectors, which are mandated on NASCAR ignition harnesses, and the Deutsch connectors. Weatherpak connectors have been used for years on OEM applications, and they hold up well. There are a number of different connectors available that will accept anywhere from a single wire to up to six wires. Each wire has its own seal and barrel, so they cannot short to the terminal next to them. The connectors also lock together resulting in a sealed and locked connection.

As we mentioned before, wiring takes patience, and when you're using Weatherpak connectors, you'll need it. You'll also need an official crimp tool that can crimp the unique terminals correctly. There are several versions available on the market, ranging from high-dollar ones, which do a terrific job, to parts-shop models that you should stay away from. MSD offers a crimp tool called the Pro-Crimp, which is supplied with crimp dies for spark plug wires. Different style dies can be installed in the tool, and they offer sets for the Weatherpak and Deutsch connectors. Once the Weatherpak connectors are assembled, you'll also need a special tool to remove each terminal, in case there's ever a need to repair a wire.

The Deutsch connectors are relatively new to the aftermarket side of performance. MSD has been using them on their Pro Mags for years, and now supplies them on their programmable ignition controls. These connectors have a lot in common with the Weatherpaks, as they also lock together and are completely sealed. They also require special crimp tools for assembly. One advantage to these connectors is that they can be disassembled with no special tools.

Soldering

If you need to make a more permanent connection between wires, such as when adding length to them, soldering them is the best method. Twisting wires together does not cut it in the world of

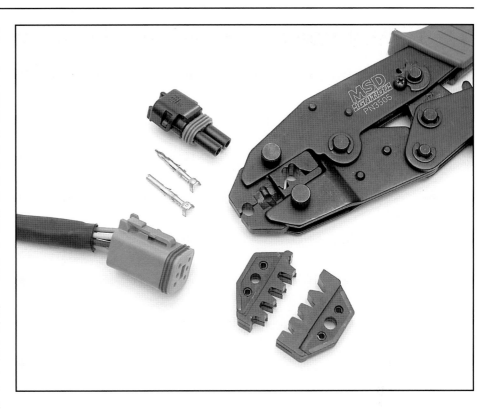

MSD's Pro-Crimp Tool is a ratcheting-style crimp tool that can be used for a variety of crimping jobs with its replaceable dies. They come with spark plug wire crimps, but MSD offers Amp pin jaws, or Weatherpak and Deutsch crimp dies for them as well.

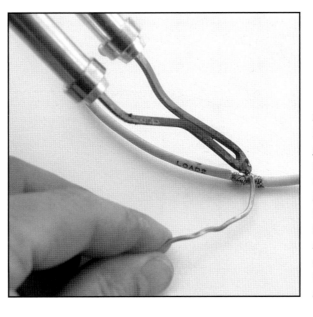

Soldering wire connections is still the best connection you can make between two wires. Always twist the wires together then apply heat directly to the wires. Once the solder melts when touched to the wires, let it smoothly flow in and around the wire strands. Once the connection cools, seal it with electrical tape.

performance. That's not even acceptable on a street car! When you're wiring for performance, you cannot afford a loose a connection or even worse, have it making sporadic connections. Finding a flat out open or short is much easier than searching for an erratic condition! Butt-splice connectors are acceptable in certain cases, such as when that section

of wire gets moved around, stretched, or pulled; but soldering wires is the best route.

Soldering two wires is the best way to join them together. The connection is solid and acts as an efficient conductor, since the solder is an alloy of tin and lead. The one downfall is that the connection is a bit brittle, so know where

Too Many Connections?

On EFI-equipped cars, there's a long list of connections that need to be pulled off during an engine swap. Then, when putting the engine back in, all of these wires need to be reconnected. When you're thrashing between rounds, a lot of bad things can happen when there's an excessive amount of connectors to deal with. A wiring specialty shop called Wires and Pliers takes all of these connectors and combines them into one convenient harness and connector.

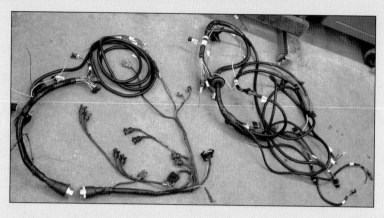

The front half of the aftermarket EFI harness that connects to the engine sensors and injectors is coiled up on the right in this photo. The entire modified harness is on the left. That's a lot of connecting!

Wires and Pliers routes all of the EFI sensor and injector wiring into one multi-terminal ITT-Cannon connector that screws into its mate, which can be mounted to the firewall. When the engine has to come out, you only have to pull one connector to do the job! This saves a lot of time and takes the chance of wiring mismatches or breaking important terminal connections out of the picture. This system would probably lend itself useful even on carbureted cars, especially with multiple nitrous systems.

Here's the ITT-Cannon Connector. When the engine needs to come out, there's only one connector to pull! If you have a multi-engine program, being prepared with two harnesses would be the way to go!

this wire connection is going to be placed and how it will be used before soldering. Also note that there are several different solder materials available. Most wiring can be handled with a rosin-core material and you can even get it with flux (a kind of the primer) already in the rosin. Aluminum, nickel, or galvanized materials will require an acid-core solder.

Relays

While we're knee deep in wiring information, this is a good time to bring up the use of relays. A relay is a switch that lets a small wire with low voltage be used to activate a circuit that requires high voltage and current through a bigger wire. Examples of where a relay is required are with the fuel pump, an electric fan, or a nitrous solenoid. When these components are initially switched on, there is a larger draw for a moment on top of the fact that they already pull a lot of current.

MSD offers two relays that are rated up to 30 amps each with an input of 12 volts. There is a Single-Pole Single-Throw model, which is ideal for single stage nitrous systems. The other model is a Double-Pole Double-Throw model that can supply high voltage and current to two components.

Relays have two separate circuits internally. One is the switch and the other acts as the controller. When the controller side is energized through the low current side, it creates a magnetic field inside the relay that controls the switching side. The switching side either activates or deactivates a high-current circuit through a normally open (NO) or normally closed (NC) switch.

There are many uses for relays, from horns to headlights to air shifter solenoids. Once you wire one and see how nice they function, you'll be hooked.

When you're wiring your ignition or any circuits in your car, it is always a good idea to take notes as to where a circuit is connected and with what color wires. This is especially true with relays and other switches. Like mapping out a plan for installing ignition parts, knowing how your relays are installed and when they're supposed to be functioning will help you in times of repair or troubleshooting.

TROUBLE SHOOTING A CD IGNITION CONTROL

It seems that the ignition system is generally the first thing that is suspected whenever a race engine hesitates or burbles going down the track. Considering all of the different components that must work in sync to perform correctly, perhaps a little guilt is warranted, that is, until the control is proven innocent. This may seem like kind of backwards thinking, but since when does an ignition have rights?

I've seen too many guys in the pits swap out ignition boxes and the coil, only to have the exact same problem. And they still come in the pits to blame the ignition! Heads up racers: if you swap parts and still have the problem, it's time to look somewhere else! Not everyone has spare parts in their trailer, but there are testers available that let you simulate running the ignition without taking anything apart.

Mallory and MSD offer handy testers that easily connect to the ignition's trigger input wire to make the ignition think the engine is running. These come with a spark plug load tool that you connect to the coil wire and ground. This test plug puts a load on the coil so it has to develop around 30,000 volts to jump the gap. If no spark occurs, connect a different coil and try again. If there's now a spark, the coil is at fault. If there's still no spark, the ignition control may be at fault. Check and make sure it is properly grounded, that it has battery voltage on the thick red wire, and that there is 12 volts on the small red on/off wire.

Another cool thing about this tester is that it has multiple features to it. Since it has an accurate digital readout of the engine RPM, you can test the accuracy of your tachometer, the shift-light operation, rev limiters, or even RPM-activated switches. Anything that is running off the tach output of the ignition will be simulated, which helpful in setting up rev limits, shift points, and switches.

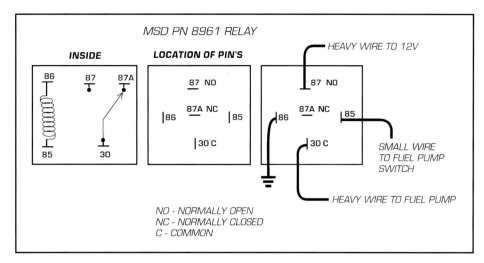

This schematic shows the internal wiring of a SPST relay. An example of wiring a fuel pump would be to connect a 14-gauge wire to the fuel pump on terminal 30 and the source wire to the normally open (NO) terminal 87. Ground for the relay is found on 86, and a small 12-volt on/off wire connects to 85. When the relay is energized through terminals 85 and 86, the armature of the relay is switched over to complete a circuit between 87 and 30 to feed the high current to the fuel pump.

An ignition tester will save you time, money, and headaches. These hand-held testers send the ignition a trigger signal to trick it into firing just as if the engine were running. You get to control the RPM, and you can even check the RPM limits, switch activation, and the tach.

If you are using a timing accessory like a retard box, trigger the tester through the control so you can check that it is also working properly. If there no spark occurs, bypass the control and trigger the tester through the ignition control. If a spark occurs, then the problem has been isolated to the acces-

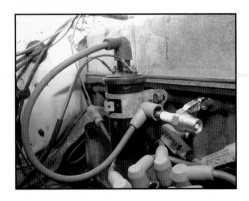

With the ignition off, pull the coil wire off the distributor cap, connect it to the test plug, and clip it to ground. A high-voltage spark will be needed to jump the gap so you can tell if the ignition and coil are pulling their weight. After running the tester, this thing will be hot, so be careful when taking it off.

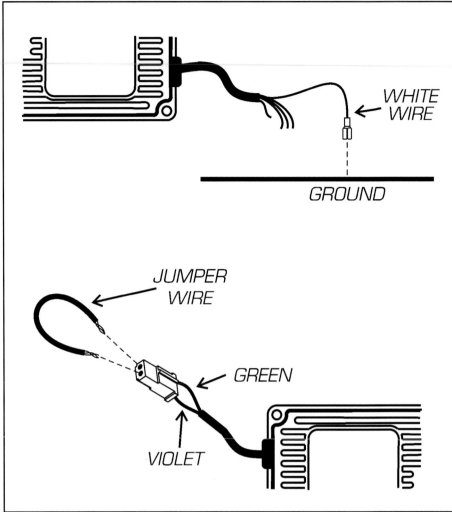

These diagrams illustrate how to fool the ignition control into firing the coil. Remove the coil wire from the distributor and place it close to a ground. When you fake trigger the ignition, a spark will jump to ground. If your car won't start for some reason this quick test will confirm that the ignition is working, and you can move to other systems.

sory or its wiring. Check the connections to the trigger source and its output signal wire to the ignition control before laying on the guilt. Remember, about half the ignition problems that occur are due to poor wiring.

If the ignition and coil check out okay, you'll need to confirm the operation of your trigger source. This gets a little tougher, since there's not much you can check other than resistance on the pickup. Most pickups have proven to be very reliable, so check the wiring and connections going to the ignition control. The other area that needs to be checked is the secondary side components. Are the rotor tip and cap terminals in good condition? What about the plug wires? Closely check their condition and even check their resistance. Remember, they're not all going to be exact. A bad wire should stand out among the group with very high resistance, or even register an open! Also, don't forget to check the plugs themselves.

The No Tester Test

An ignition tester is a great tool, but not everyone is going to have one in their tool box (though it is highly recommended for racers). There are still other ways to check the operation of your CD ignition control and coil just

to make sure they're doing their job. This test is generally more helpful on no-start conditions, as you won't be able to run any RPM, well maybe a 10 or 20 rpm, but at least you can confirm that a spark occurs.

With the ignition off, remove the coil wire from the distributor cap. Position it so it is within a 1/2 inch away from a ground. Next, disconnect the trigger source from the distributor or crank trigger pickup. Now, turn the ignition on, but don't crank the engine. If you are using the single wire input of the ignition control, take that wire and tap it to ground several times. You are going to stand in for the trigger signal.

Every time the wire is removed from ground, a spark should jump from the coil wire to ground. In the case of a magnetic pickup being used, jump the two wires together with a paper clip or piece of wire, and then break the connection. When this occurs, a spark should jump from the coil wire to ground.

When the ignition checks okay, it leads to questions about grounds, battery supply, and of course, the wiring. Once the ignition and electrical system are cleared of being at fault, it's time to look into fuel supply and delivery systems, and then on to mechanical components in the engine. Good luck!

DEFINITIONS AND DIAGRAMS
Useful Info and Wiring Schematics

Now that we're pretty much at the end of the book, you should have a much better grasp on what you need to really make your car fire up. As you search through catalogs, websites, and ads, you're going to notice that there are output numbers and specifications given for just about anything used in an ignition system. The specifications are there, but the explanations of each measurement generally aren't, so we figured listing some of the more common measurements and what they refer to would be a helpful way to wrap up a discussion about performance ignitions.

There are three main ingredients so to speak when it comes to electricity in an automotive ignition system: voltage, current, and resistance.

Voltage: This is an electrical force that causes current to flow through a circuit or conductor. Its specification is given in volts (v).

Current: This refers to the flow of electrons through a conductor. It is measured in amps (a).

Resistance: Resistance is just that — opposition to the flow of current. It is measured in ohms.

We can use a hose, faucet, and water as a crude analogy of the working rela-tionship between voltage, current, and resistance. Voltage is the water pressure going through the hose. The more pres-sure, the more water gets through the hose, just as more voltage would send more current through a conductor. The faucet can be described as the resistance. As you close the faucet, you're increas-ing the resistance to the flow, causing a reduction. When it's open, the flow increases.

Ohms Law: You may hear about Ohm's law occasionally, and not from a cop after an "exhibition of speed." Ohm's law is a formula that helps figure out an unknown in an electrical circuit when two of the main three are known. It states that amperage varies in a direct ratio to voltage (amperage increases as voltage increases) while it is inversely proportional to resistance (amperage decreases as resistance increases). The formula uses E over IR, where E=Volt-age, I=Amps, and R=Resistance.

Operating Voltage: This is the amount of voltage that the ignition control requires to operate at its full potential. Most ignition controls are designed to operate at full output with 10 – 18 volts. Once the voltage dips below 10 volts, the engine will keep running but the ignition will not be operating at its full potential and engine performance will

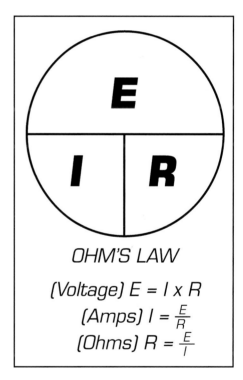

OHM'S LAW

$(Voltage)\ E = I \times R$

$(Amps)\ I = \dfrac{E}{R}$

$(Ohms)\ R = \dfrac{E}{I}$

The infamous pie chart that is Ohm's law. You can figure out the voltage, current, or resistance of a circuit by plug-ging in two values. This can be handy when building different circuits or figur-ing out voltage and current require-ments.

begin to decline. This is why it is so important to have a fully charged bat-tery in cases when a charging system is not used.

Operating Current: The current or amperage that a CD ignition control draws is extremely important. As engine RPM increases, the ignition draws more current from the battery in order to produce more output. The thing to keep in mind here is that you may have a lot of other circuits pulling current from the battery as well. Water pumps, fuel pumps, nitrous solenoids, electric fans, and other accessories use current and they will also generally increase their draw as RPM increases. Be sure to have a charging system or battery that can meet the current demands of your system. For inductive ignition systems, this refers to the maximum amount of current that is going into the coil.

Output Voltage: This specification, also called secondary voltage, is a meas-ure of how much voltage is produced through the secondary windings of the coil. This is the most common specification used to judge coils, and perhaps the most misinterpreted as well. When you see a coil that is rated at 50,000 volts, that is referring to its output potential. It could handle that amount of voltage, though in the real world it will probably never see 50,000 volts. Remember, an ignition only uses as much voltage as it needs to jump the plug gap, and rarely will that ever require 50,000 volts. Not to mention, the secondary side of the ignition really won't be able to handle that amount of voltage.

There are also a lot of variables that determine output voltage: the ignition type being used, the coil turns ratio, the energy of the ignition, the construction of the coil, and more. It is important to have a good quality coil that is capable of delivering high voltage when it needs to.

Spark Energy: This is a measure of how much 'heat' is produced at the spark plug gap. It is a product of voltage, current, and time. It is measured in joules, or millijoules in most ignition cases. Inductive ignitions use this to indicate the amount of energy that is stored in the coil.

Spark Duration: The spark duration is how long the spark burns in the cylinder. Some companies list this as the amount of time that the multiple sparks occur. Most multiple-sparking ignitions provide a spark series that lasts for 20° of crankshaft rotation. When this spec is mentioned in association with coils, it refers to a single spark and is listed in microseconds.

WIRING DIAGRAMS

On the next few pages you'll find a variety of wiring diagrams. These are meant to be helpful in showing you that most ignition upgrades are fairly easy to install. Whenever you're wiring in a component, it is recommended that you have the manufacturer's installation instructions. If not, all of these companies have good support departments or websites where you can download info or ask about your specific application. Check our Sources page to find out how to get in touch with each company.

Another good idea, especially when dealing with late model cars, is to have the vehicle's wiring diagram. In many cases, wires need to be traced, cut, or spliced into, and you need to be absolutely positive that you are working with the right wires. You don't want to connect 470 volts to the vehicle speed sensor!

The more information you have about your ignition components, the better off you will be when it comes to installing and tuning. Ignition instructions and catalogs contain valuable information. In this day and age with the web, faxes, and email, there is no excuse for not being informed. Be sure to read the instructions, not just look at the diagrams and photos!

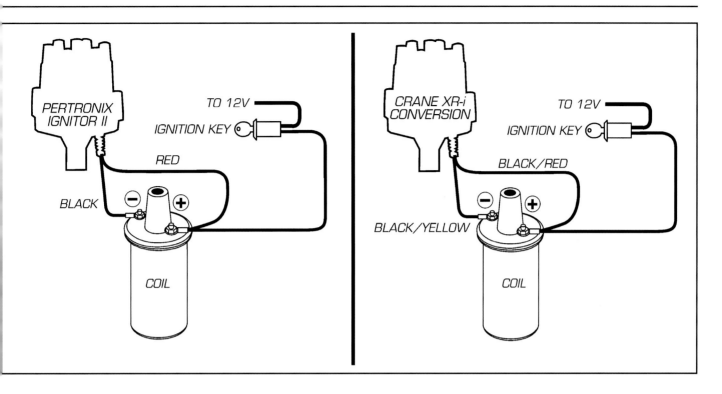

These diagrams show the wiring of two points replacement kits. These kits, from Pertronix and Crane, both install easily into your stock distributor in place of the breaker points, making adjustments and wear a thing of the past. The only sign that there are electronics inside the distributor is that there are two wires coming out. Since the kits are electronic, they require a 12-volt source.

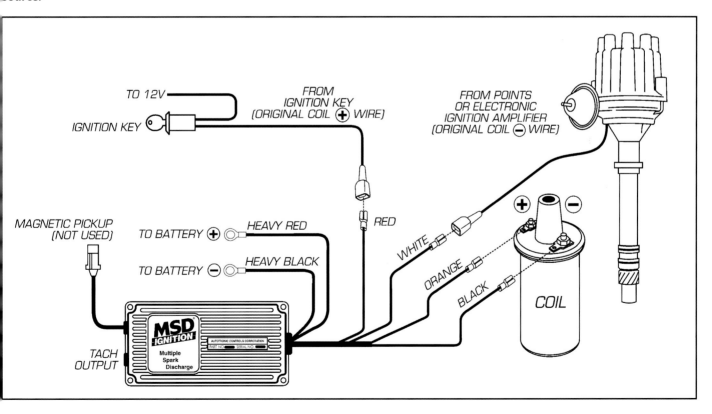

If your points distributor is in good working condition and you don't plan on revving the engine through racing-type RPM, you can run an ignition control with the stock points. The points will last longer because they're operating merely as a switching device, plus you'll get the benefits of the CD sparks from the ignition you chose.

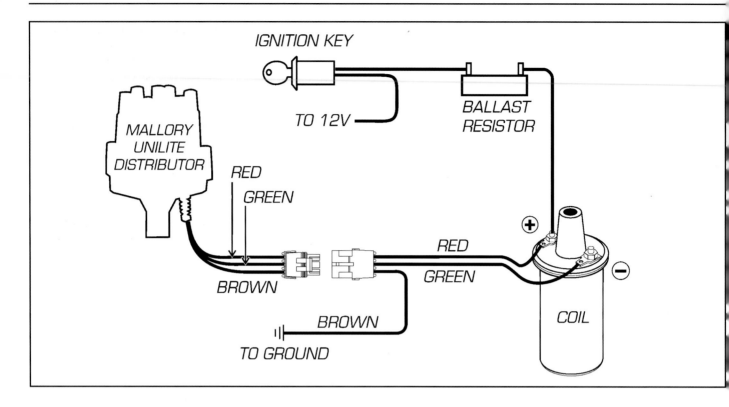

The Uni-Lite Distributor from Mallory is a popular alternative to distributors with breaker points. The electronic distributor uses a maintenance-free optical sensor to trigger the ignition. It is easy to install with only three wires to connect, plus its small housing fits in tight areas that an HEI or even a standard size housing can't. This makes them ideal for street rods.

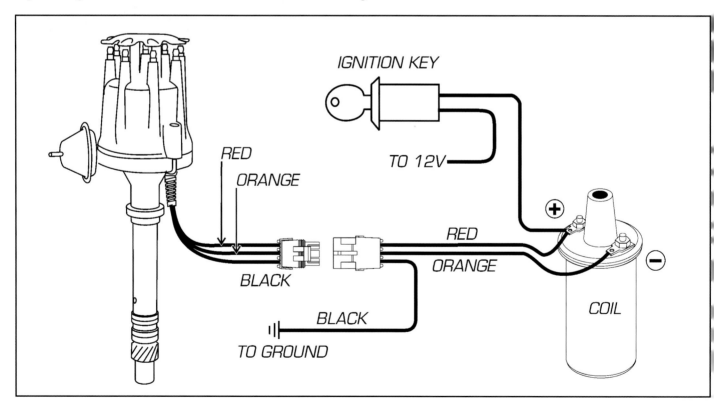

The MSD Ready-to-Run Distributor is a self-contained electronic distributor. It has an electronic module that is triggered by a magnetic pickup. The module is an inductive ignition design that connects to the coil's negative and positive terminals and a ground wire.

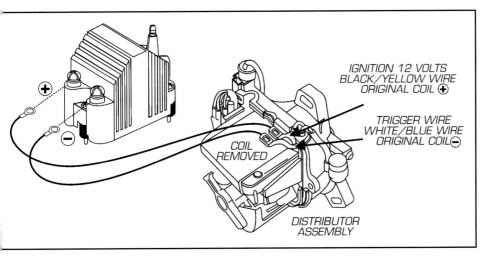

The most popular Honda and Acura engines that are being modified generally have a distributor with an internal coil. Performance ignition companies found that the internal coil can easily be removed so you can wire in a high-output external coil to spruce up the spark in the cylinder. The cap must be modified to accept a secondary coil wire by adding a terminal tower. There are also several caps available from companies that are already modified and will bolt right in place of the stock version.

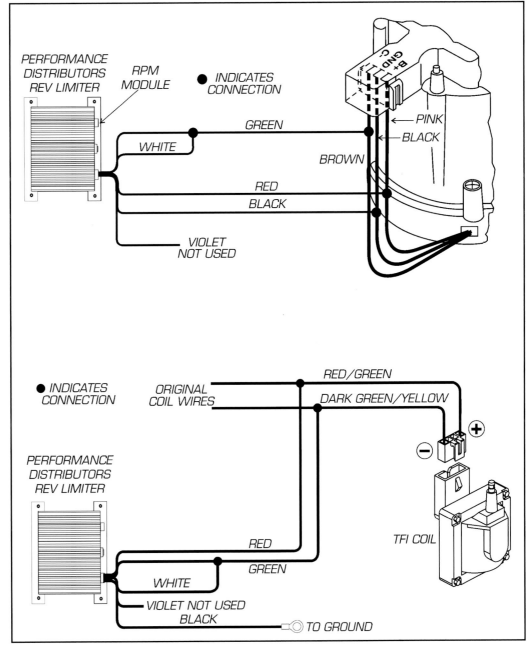

If you don't run a fancy ignition control but still want to have a rev limiter on your engine, Performance Distributors offers a rev control that operates with factory inductive ignition systems. As you can see, the control is easy to install, and the RPM limits are adjusted with popular plug-in modules.

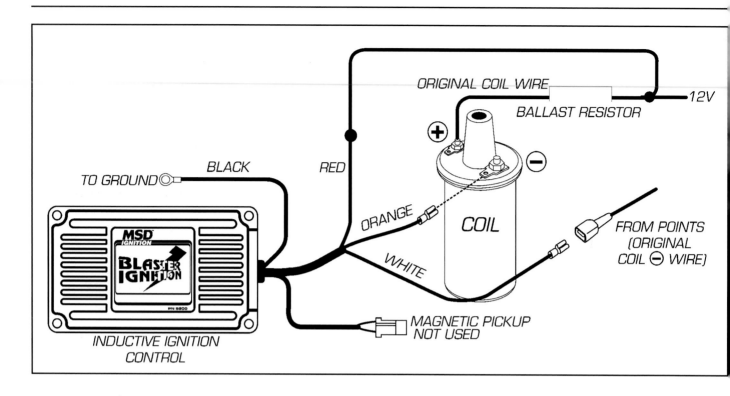

If you're looking for just a little more oomph from your engine while staying within a budget, there are several inductive ignitions that fit the bill. Most of these controls put a little more current to the coil while improving the dwell control of the ignition. Installation is simple, with only a trigger source, 12-volt input, and a coil negative connection.

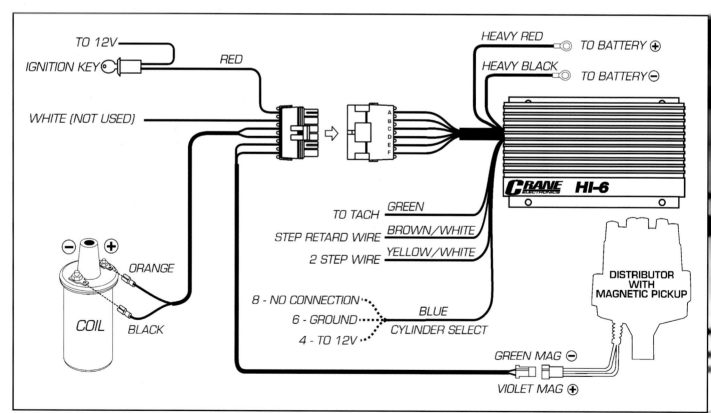

For the most part, all of the multiple-sparking capacitive discharge ignitions install the same way. It is important to note that the only wires that connect to the coil primary terminals come from the ignition! Never connect a test light, tach or other accessories to the coil terminals with a CD ignition. This diagram shows a Fireball HI-6 wired to a distributor with a magnetic pickup.

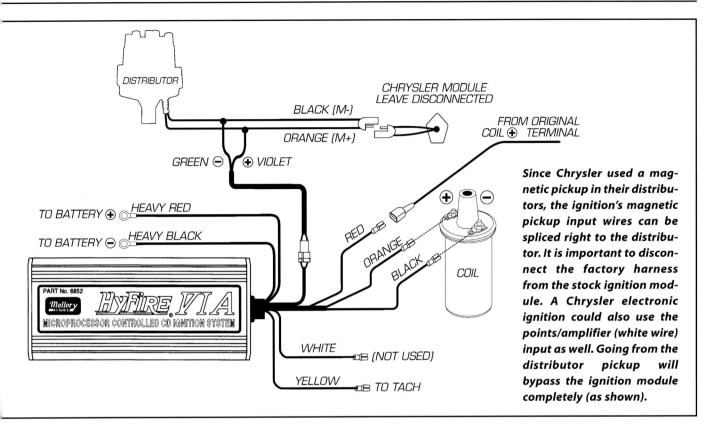

DISTRIBUTOR

CHRYSLER MODULE
LEAVE DISCONNECTED

BLACK (M-)

ORANGE (M+)

FROM ORIGINAL
COIL ⊕ TERMINAL

GREEN ⊖   ⊕ VIOLET

TO BATTERY ⊕   HEAVY RED

TO BATTERY ⊖   HEAVY BLACK

RED

ORANGE

BLACK

COIL

PART No. 6852

Mallory

HyFire VIA

MICROPROCESSOR CONTROLLED CD IGNITION SYSTEM

WHITE   ⊐B (NOT USED)

YELLOW   ⊐B TO TACH

Since Chrysler used a magnetic pickup in their distributors, the ignition's magnetic pickup input wires can be spliced right to the distributor. It is important to disconnect the factory harness from the stock ignition module. A Chrysler electronic ignition could also use the points/amplifier (white wire) input as well. Going from the distributor pickup will bypass the ignition module completely (as shown).

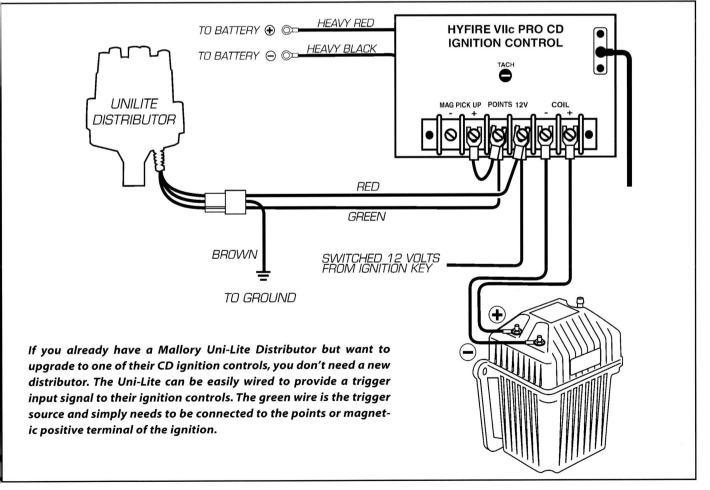

TO BATTERY ⊕   HEAVY RED

TO BATTERY ⊖   HEAVY BLACK

**HYFIRE VIIc PRO CD
IGNITION CONTROL**

TACH

MAG PICK UP   POINTS 12V   COIL
  -      +   -   +

UNILITE
DISTRIBUTOR

RED

GREEN

BROWN

SWITCHED 12 VOLTS
FROM IGNITION KEY

TO GROUND

If you already have a Mallory Uni-Lite Distributor but want to upgrade to one of their CD ignition controls, you don't need a new distributor. The Uni-Lite can be easily wired to provide a trigger input signal to their ignition controls. The green wire is the trigger source and simply needs to be connected to the points or magnetic positive terminal of the ignition.

Wiring an Ignition Control to an HEI

Even though they haven't been offered on a new car in nearly two decades, the GM HEI is one of the most popular distributors available. Many new crate engines are supplied with a brand new HEI distributor, and most ignition companies offer accessories and even complete HEI distributors.

When GM was producing the HEI, there were a couple different versions. When you're upgrading your ignition, you'll need to know which model HEI you are using in order to complete the installation correctly. The difference between the HEIs has to do with the number of terminals that the ignition module has: four, five, or seven. The four-pin version will have a vacuum advance canister. It is the most popular. The five- and seven-pin models came on later model vehicles and incorporated a knock sensor or some sort of electronic timing control. The installations will vary by either using the magnetic pickup of the ignition or its points/amplifier input. Also, the HEI module may be used or removed from the housing.

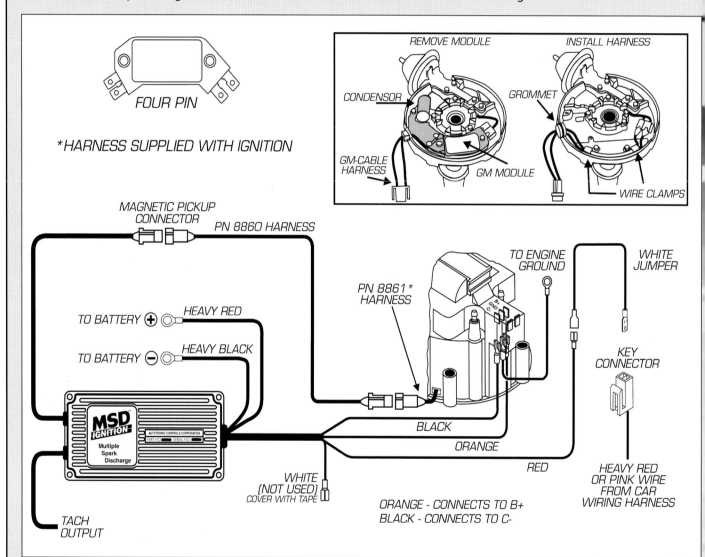

When you have a four-pin HEI module (shown at the top of the diagram), it must be completely removed in order to connect a CD ignition control. With the module removed, a small harness is connected to the trigger pickup and routed to the ignition's magnetic pickup connector. Notice that the white wire of the ignition control is not used.

Wiring an Ignition Control to an HEI

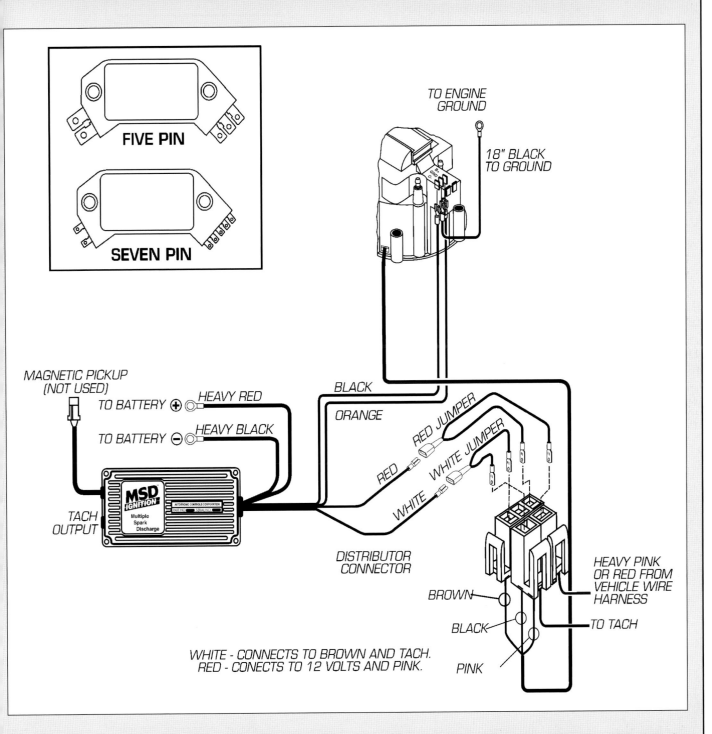

FIVE PIN

SEVEN PIN

TO ENGINE GROUND

18" BLACK TO GROUND

MAGNETIC PICKUP (NOT USED)

TO BATTERY ⊕ — HEAVY RED

TO BATTERY ⊖ — HEAVY BLACK

BLACK

ORANGE

RED JUMPER

RED

WHITE JUMPER

WHITE

MSD IGNITION
Multiple Spark Discharge

TACH OUTPUT

DISTRIBUTOR CONNECTOR

HEAVY PINK OR RED FROM VEHICLE WIRE HARNESS

BROWN

BLACK

TO TACH

PINK

WHITE - CONNECTS TO BROWN AND TACH.
RED - CONECTS TO 12 VOLTS AND PINK.

An HEI that uses a five- or seven-pin module will use the single white wire trigger for points or amplifiers, rather than the magnetic pickup. Generally these distributors can be identified by their lack of a vacuum advance canister, though some five-pin models retain the canister. For these installations, the module stays in the distributor and the trigger signal comes through the module.

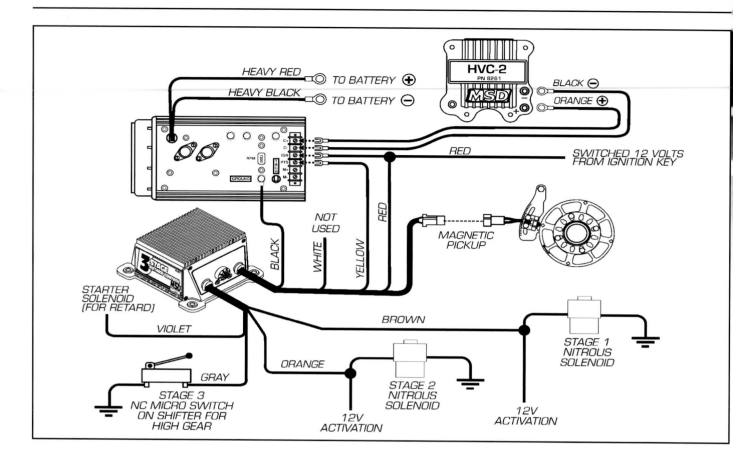

Adding a timing accessory control box is easy. Just remember that the timing control must always be wired before the ignition. There will be two inputs on the timing accessory for points/amplifier or magnetic pickup, just like the ignition control. Then there will be an output that connects to the ignition's points/amplifier input wire. This diagram shows a complete multi-step retard wiring on an MSD 7AL-2 system.

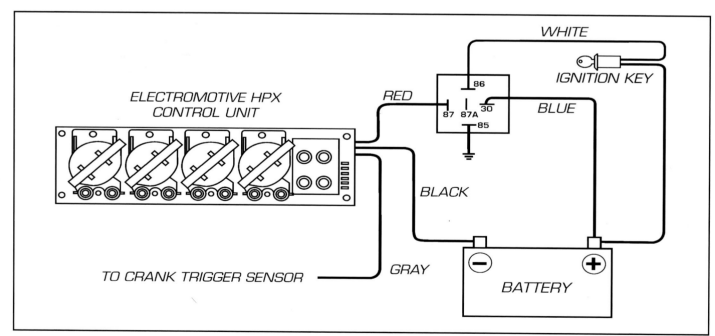

The Electromotive HPX Ignition is a whole different ball game with its dual-output coils and conspicuously absent distributor. However, the ignition is almost too easy to wire and install! This diagram shows the installation with a relay, so there is will be no draw when the key is off. The relay isn't necessary in all installations.

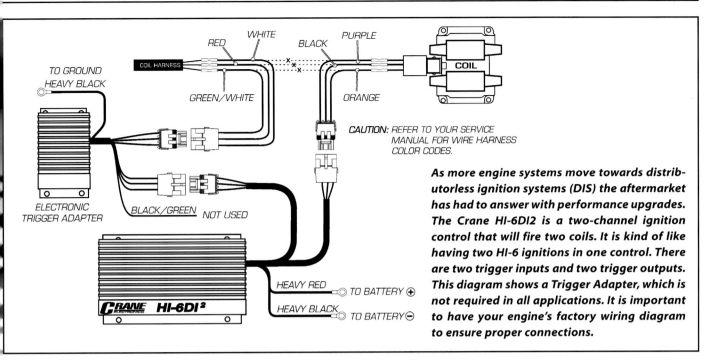

As more engine systems move towards distributorless ignition systems (DIS) the aftermarket has had to answer with performance upgrades. The Crane HI-6DI2 is a two-channel ignition control that will fire two coils. It is kind of like having two HI-6 ignitions in one control. There are two trigger inputs and two trigger outputs. This diagram shows a Trigger Adapter, which is not required in all applications. It is important to have your engine's factory wiring diagram to ensure proper connections.

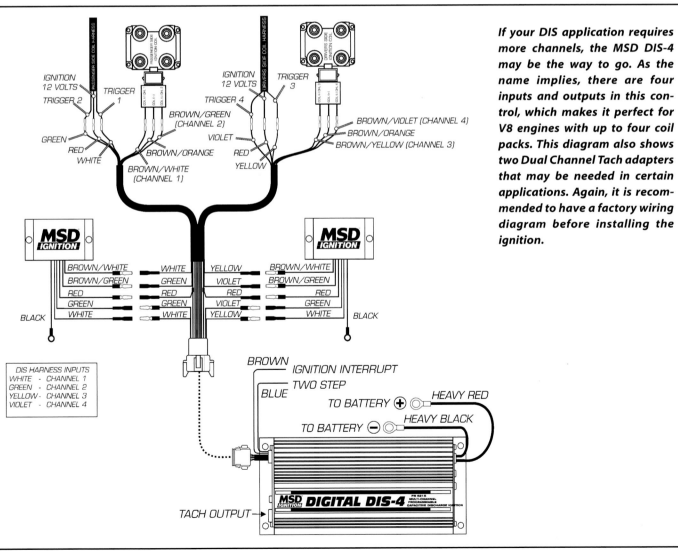

If your DIS application requires more channels, the MSD DIS-4 may be the way to go. As the name implies, there are four inputs and outputs in this control, which makes it perfect for V8 engines with up to four coil packs. This diagram also shows two Dual Channel Tach adapters that may be needed in certain applications. Again, it is recommended to have a factory wiring diagram before installing the ignition.

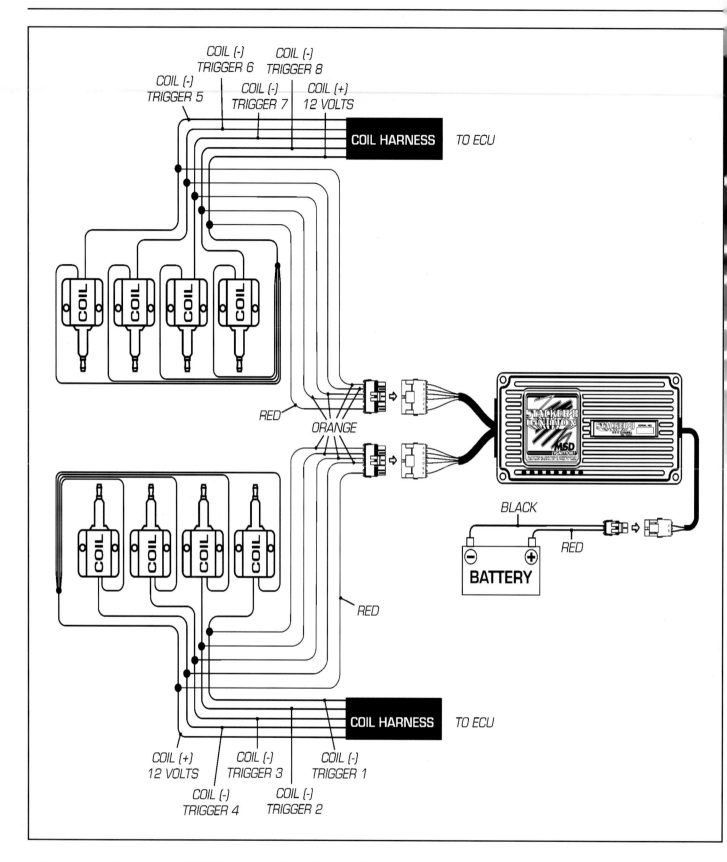

In the past couple years, the OEM's have moved to coil-per-cylinder or coil-on-plug ignition systems. This can present a challenge to the ignition companies in that they now need eight channels! MSD offers one ignition, the Stacker 8, which will put a CD spark on top of the factory inductive ignition spark to improve the performance of the ignition. If the factory ignition system has the current controlling drive circuits built into the coils, this ignition cannot be used. Find out before you buy!

SOURCE GUIDE

Autolite – Honeywell
39 Old Ridgebury Road
Danbury, CT 06810
www.autolite.com

Crane Cams
530 Fentress Blvd.
Daytona Beach, FL 32114
Phone: (386) 252-1151
Fax: (386) 258-6167
www.cranecams.com

Denso
3900 Via Oro Avenue
Long Beach, CA 90810
(888) 963-3676
www.denso-dsca.com

Electromotive
9131 Cetreville Road
Manassas, VA 20110-5208
(703) 331-0100
www.electromotive-inc.com

Fire Control Ignition Systems
2519 Dana Drive.
Laurinburg, NC 28352
(866) 282-0620
www.fcignition.com

Holley Performance Products
1801 Russellville Road
Bowling Green, KY 42101
(270) 782-2900
Fax: (270) 782-1988
www.holley.com

Jesel
1985 Cedarbridge Avenue
Lakewood, New Jersey 08701
(732) 901-1800
www.jesel.com

Mallory
550 Mallory Way
Carson City, NV 89701
(775) 882-6600
www.mrgasket.com

Moroso
80 Carter Drive,
Guilford CT 06437-0570
(203) 453-6571
www.moroso.com

Mr. Gasket/Accel
10601 Memphis Ave., #12
Cleveland, OH 44144
Phone: (216) 688-8300
Fax: (216) 688-8305
www.mrgasket.com

MSD Ignition
1490 Henry Brennan Dr.
El Paso, TX 79936
(915) 857-5200
www.msdignition.com

Optima Batteries
17500 East 22nd Avenue
Aurora, CA 80011
(303) 340-7440
www.optimabatteries.com

Performance Distributors
2699 Barris Drive
Memphis, TN 38132
(901) 396-5782
www.performancedistributors.com

Pertronix
440 East Arrow Highway
San Dimas, CA 91773
Phone: (800) 827-3758
Fax: (909) 599-6424
www.pertronix.com

PowerMaster
2401 Dutch Valley Drive
Knoxville, TN 37918
(865) 688-5953
www.powermastermotorsports.com

Turbostart
3601 Willmington Road
New Castle, PA 16105
(724) 658-5501
www.turbostart.com